WHAT WORKS
FOR SINGLES

FOR RELATIONSHIPS
FOR MARRIAGE
FOR LIFE

Solid Choices in Unstable Times

D0980689

WHAT WORKS for Singles

Published by *El Paseo Publications*

Design and Composition by *Scan Communications Group, Inc., Dubuque, IA*

Produced by *Central Plains Book Manufacturing, Winfield, KS*

All Biblical references, unless specified otherwise, were obtained from the Spirit Filled Life Bible (New King James version). Executive editor, Pastor Jack Hayford. Published by THOMAS NELSON, 1995.

We make every effort to attribute the source of quotes to the correct author. If there is no acknowledgement, the author either wrote the quote or we could not determine the source. If you can identify the source, we encourage you to contact us.

ISBN: 0-9713393-2-5

Library of Congress Control Number: 2003091369

Printed in the United States of America
10 9 8 7 6 5 4 3 2 1

DEDICATION

This book is dedicated to my beautiful wife, Morgan Idleman, and to my mother, Diane Idleman, who has been there for me throughout the years.

Thank you Morgan for believing in me and in this book, and thank you for sharing your experience at the end of the book. And thank you Mom for the many days, nights, weeks and months invested—may it return a hundredfold; I could not have completed it without your love and support.

BOOK #2 FROM THE
WHAT WORKS BOOK SERIES

E.P.

EL PASEO PUBLICATIONS

WHAT WORKS for Singles was written based on personal experience and observation, and is sold with that understanding. The purpose of this resource is not to replace other books containing similar information, but to complement them. You are encouraged to learn as much as possible by reading other reputable books. A brief list of notable authors is listed in the notes section in the back of the book. The Bible provides the primary source of information.

El Paseo Publications is committed to quality in publication—to inspire, educate and encourage the highest standard of excellence through written communication.

What Do Pastors Have to Say about WHAT WORKS for Singles . . .

When Shane Idleman was asked to speak to the *Antelope Valley Christian Ministerial Association* on the topic of health and fitness in Southern California, he met pastors from a variety of churches and denominations who positively responded to his message. Several of the pastors have recommended *WHAT WORKS for Singles;* a limited number of comments are listed below . . .

WHAT WORKS for Singles . . . gives values to the dating process, offers a practical guide in preparing for a healthy marriage and provides a solid foundation for lasting relationships; I highly recommend this resource.
Senior Pastor, Sean Appleton
Quartz Hill Foursquare Church, Quartz Hill, CA

As the father of two teenage daughters who are focused on doing life and relationships right, this book was both a supportive companion and a challenging voice of conviction for my "singles" and me. I recommend it passionately, urgently and wholeheartedly . . .
Pastor Jim Girdlestone
The Desert Vineyard Church, Lancaster, CA

WHAT WORKS for Singles . . . offers meaningful insight into how biblical principles can deepen relationships at every level. Here is a doable, genuinely useful guide to Christian dating and the preparation for deeper Christian relationships. The ideas presented in *What Works for Singles* . . . are simple, clear, and easy to grasp—yet profound in their implications. I recommend you read it with an open, seeking heart.
Senior Pastor, Ken Hart (Supervisor of the High Desert District of Foursquare Churches)
The Highlands Church, Palmdale, CA

WHAT WORKS for Singles . . . places value on both the marriage commitment and the Word of God. It challenges us all to lead more productive, Christ-centered lives. If you purchase just one relationship book this year, I suggest this one.
Senior Pastor, James Majeske
First Assembly of God Church, Lancaster, CA

Many singles have searched for good, sound biblical teaching and information that will lead to a more productive single life, and help prepare them for a Christ-centered marriage—I highly recommend *WHAT WORKS for Singles*. . .
Senior Pastor, Tom Pickens
Antelope Valley Christian Center, Lancaster, CA
Former President of Antelope Valley Christian Ministerial Association

WHAT WORKS for Singles . . . encourages singles to embrace God's plan for their lives no matter what state they are in relationally. It can help singles, and those married, avoid relationship failure, and show them how to turn past brokenness into stepping-stones to success.
Senior Pastor, Dave Prather
Central Christian Church, Lancaster, CA

The "single life" is a place where millions live everyday. Shane Idleman insightfully describes its thoughts, aspirations and struggles. And best of all, he's pointed out, practically and biblically, what it takes to live healthier, happier lives as you date, or plan to marry. This is a must read book for anyone who is single.
Pastor David Sill
Higher Ground/Central Christian Church, Lancaster, CA

WHAT WORKS for Singles . . . provides fuel for the believer who is serious about long-term transformation; biblical principles are the foundation for practical and victorious Christian living; a must read!
Senior Pastor, Jan Spencer
Living Way Church, Lancaster, CA

WHAT WORKS for Singles . . . is a wonderful tool to help people discover Biblical principles about marriage and relationships. Shane Idleman is transparent and insightful as he shares practical advice for people who want to build loving, lifelong marriages.
Cecil Swetland
Executive Director, Desert Christian Schools, Lancaster, CA

THE AUTHOR'S ACKNOWLEDGMENTS

First and foremost, I want to thank God for inspiration and guidance. As I look back over the years, I'm reminded of II Corinthians 4:8–9: "We are hard-pressed on every side, yet not crushed; we are perplexed, but not in despair; persecuted, but not forsaken; struck down, but not destroyed." When I was hard pressed, I was molded into the person He intended me to be. When I was perplexed, I had only to ask for direction and move forward. When I was persecuted, I found hope through spiritual truths. When I was struck down, clearly God restored me; and when I wanted to give up, I found the endless encouragement to continue.

My mother, Diane Idleman, has continued to offer guidance, encouragement, leadership, integrity and an overall positive attitude toward challenges. When I found myself in battles difficult to face, it was her compassion, understanding and constant reference to God's Word that preserved me. Not only is she a great mother, but an exceptional editor and "book doctor"; I could not have done it on my own. Thank you for the many days, nights, weeks and months invested—may it return a hundred fold. Aside from the Lord, in the words of Abraham Lincoln, *"All that I am, and all that I'll ever be, I owe to my mother!"*

A special thanks to my brother, Ryan, and his wife, Christina, along with Christian and Austin, and my sister, Meredith—all have been a tremendous support. Challenges created by the *WHAT WORKS Book Series* have brought us closer together. I thank God for family members who add to life rather than take from it. Thanks to my Aunt Pauline, for her patience in reviewing this material, often with very little notice.

I want to thank my wife, Morgan Idleman, who was a tremendous support. Her unconditional love removed walls built from the past and held our relationship together during the difficult times. I thank her for believing in me and in this book. I also want to thank Morgan's family for their support and acceptance: Augie, Linda, Leah, Curt, Jessy and Allison.

I began by acknowledging my heavenly Father and it seems fitting to end with my biological father. Jim Idleman, who died of a heart attack at an early age of fifty-four, inspired me more than he could have known. Qualities such as honesty, integrity, commitment, discipline and a very strong work ethic are not easily taught. *Values are not transmitted through mere words; they are instilled through a life that models these traits.* I learned many things through his example, and I'll be forever grateful for the experiences we shared, the lessons I learned and the man I became as a result of the time we spent together.

Thanks to pastors Sean and Kay Appleton, and Jim Girdlestone for their review of the manuscript, and for their counsel and godly advice. A special thanks to the pastors in my area who were a tremendous support and encouragement during this project . . . David Sill, Ken Hart, Dave Prather, Tom Pickens, James Majeske, Jan Spencer and Dave Parker.

Thanks to Ty and Julie Dripps, Erin and Russ Karsten, Renee and Dan Elkins, Stephen Hampton, Robin Blakely and Heather Horning for their insightful comments and suggestions.

Though not aware of their influence via the media, several others have provided spiritual fortification and fuel for the completion of this book. My thanks to Dr. James Dobson, Bishop T.D. Jakes, Charles Stanley, Chuck Swindoll, Chuck Smith, Jack Hayford, James MacDonald and those on The Calvary Satellite Network, The Living Way Radio Network, Focus on the Family, Family Life Today and Promise Keepers, to name only a few.

ABOUT THE AUTHOR

WHAT WORKS When "Diets" Don't was the first book written by Shane Idleman, and the first in the *WHAT WORKS Books Series.*

Although physical health has been his focus—promoting spiritual health is his greatest desire. His passion for God's Word may well have been planted nearly 400 years ago when the Pilgrims first set foot on American soil. Interestingly enough, Shane's maternal grandfather's lineage can be traced to Peregrine White, the first baby born on the Mayflower in Cape Cod Bay. As the *Mayflower Compact* was signed, members present no doubt prayed that God would bless America, and that their children and grandchildren would carry biblical principles into each new generation. Shane not only believes that his desire to uphold God-given spiritual absolutes in this generation is God's desire for each of us, but, more personally, it may be in answer to that prayer spoken nearly 400 years ago in the early hours of American history.

Today, God's wisdom has all but been removed from social norms. Scripture requires that we stand on our commitments, on our integrity and on our values. Idleman states that although many believe that the battle is too advanced to make a difference, he believes that we can reverse the trend, and offers this book as his contribution to that commitment.

As a Southern California corporate executive for the world's fastest growing fitness company, Shane had the opportunity to work with, and interview well over 30,000 people. *Challenges varied; however, fundamental principles of success did not change.* For many, the ability to look beyond their circumstances and rebuild their brokenness into an unbreakable spirit depended largely on the strength of their foundation.

The ability to look beyond their circumstances and rebuild their brokenness into an unbreakable spirit depended largely on the strength of their foundation.

From this experience, and his own, Shane isolated seven biblical principles that can help overcome many of the obstacles that we face today. The information presented is not based on tests, surveys or questionnaires—it is based on life experiences from ordinary people that have developed extraordinary qualities by acknowledging certain values.

Shane is currently the C.E.O. of *WHAT WORKS, Inc.* and *WhyDietsDontWork.com.* He resides in Southern California with his wife, Morgan.

ADVISORY OVERVIEW

Morgan Idleman

Morgan Idleman, the author's wife, speaks regularly to singles and young adults regarding issues such as dating, marriage commitment, media influence and creating a healthy self-image. Shane and Morgan, now married, applied the seven biblical principles to their personal lives and relationship.

Diane Idleman

Diane Idleman, the author's mother, who was extremely instrumental in the success of *WHAT WORKS When "Diets" Don't,* provides the editorial and advisory overview of the book. She received a Bachelors and Masters Degree in Psychology, and adds several years of experience in working with families, singles and couples in crisis in Southern California. She is also a certified teacher for the University of Phoenix. Thus, the series of books draws on years of practical experience as well as professional knowledge.

NOTE FROM THE AUTHOR

As you begin, I strongly encourage you to journal. Journaling is an excellent way to give place to thoughts, release emotions and to help chart progress. Most of the information in this book, and *WHAT WORKS When "Diets" Don't,* came from my journals before they were in manuscript form. Never underestimate the importance of journaling! (For those interested, I've included a brief section at the back of the book for journaling.)

At the end of each chapter is a section entitled: *Questions to Consider.* Reflect on these questions, identify areas that may require more attention and journal your thoughts as they arise.

God placed great emphasis on written word as well as spoken word. To begin, choose a subject, perhaps on developing your character and find related Scriptures, and read the chapters in their entirety. Date your entry; note the Scripture, your thoughts, prayers and how it can be directly applied to your life. Note answers to prayers. You'll be encouraged as you reflect on God's provision throughout your life.

CONTENTS

Building the Foundation

*A strong foundation will cost something,
but a weak foundation will cost more*

Building has been booming in Southern California for as long as I can remember. Throughout my teen years, I worked with my father in the family's under-ground construction business. Contractors were very careful in preparing the ground and laying the foundation.

Although, the cost to build a strong foundation was expensive, a weak foundation could cost more. Without proper support, a structure may not be sound and could present future problems. Developers hired architects and engineers, appointed a contractor, paid fees to the county or to the city, as well as to other departments, developed a set of plans and used heavy equipment to move tons of dirt, all to prepare the foundation. In the same way, our character provides the foundation on which we build our lives and our relationships. Many singles, as well as those married, spend years rebuilding relationships simply because the foundation was weak. Make no mistake about it, *a strong foundation will cost you something, but a weak foundation will cost you more.* Companies who neglect the foundation can, in the end, spend millions of dollars reinforcing, restoring and rebuilding. In the same way, we may spend years rebuilding and restoring our lives if we neglect our foundation. Clearly, the foundation we build today provides the strength that weathers tomorrow's storm.

> *The foundation we build today provides the strength that weathers tomorrow's storm.*

It's unfortunate that society focuses largely on external factors such as looks, money, position or status. These superficial values have left our nation in a moral, and a spiritual crisis. *We've become a society focused on prosperity instead of provision, we value wealth instead of wisdom, and we are drawn to charisma instead of character.* It's little wonder that divorce is at an all time high—our foundation as a nation, and as individuals, has slowly deteriorated.

In the past, a life-long commitment and exclusive intimacy in marriage held the family together. It was in that setting that children learned and character developed. Divorce was rarely an option, and a husband or a wife was considered an asset rather than a liability. *WHAT WORKS for Singles* is intended to help develop and support strong relationships, because the choices you make today may very well be the marriage you save tomorrow.

Many times, the problem isn't that we raise our standard and miss it, it's that we lower it and hit it!

CHAPTER ONE

Principle

Choosing to Change from the Inside Out

The choices you make today can be the marriage you save tomorrow

Marriage, today, is not failing because it's more difficult than in years past—I believe it's failing because the foundation has weakened.

As a child, I was captured by the stories that my grandfather told about life on the farm in Oklahoma in the mid 1900's. The images I've held are not those of pleasant surroundings and ideal conditions; they're impressions of twelve-hour days spent

Marriage is not failing because it's more difficult—it's failing because the foundation has weakened.

working the land, wind storms that could devastate a crop, blistered and sunburned skin and poverty unlike most Americans know today. Life, in general, was harder then, but interestingly enough, character seemed much stronger. It was a time when commitment, integrity and honesty stood in place of contracts, disclosures and bylaws. I'm not suggesting that we return to that time in history, but that we learn from the past and strongly encourage those same principles today.

What do you bring into a relationship? Are you willing to develop qualities that support commitment? Many focus on *finding* the "right" person without first focusing on *becoming* the "right" person. The principle of *reaping* and *sowing* not only relates to financial success, but it relates to success with others. If one desires to find a trustworthy, honest, committed person, he or she should first offer the same. Unfortunately, character qualities such as honesty, integrity, commitment, perseverance and servitude have been compromised. As a result, *marriages, families and other relationships often fail because they embrace values that promote meeting self-centered needs rather than meeting the needs of others.*

It's no surprise that more than fifty percent of all marriages in the United States end in divorce. I believe this number would be significantly lower if basic principles were acknowledged before marriage, as well as after. Love doesn't leave people—people leave love. True love is not just an ecstatic feeling; it's a decision that we make to remain faithful to our commitment. Marriage was intended to be a commitment based on love, surrendered to service, built on

> *Love doesn't leave people—people leave love.*

perseverance and held together by commitment. A *FOCUS ON THE FAMILY* Newsletter stated that when a research team studied 5,232 married adults who were interviewed in the late 1980's, they discovered that 645 of them were unhappily married. Five years later, these same adults (some divorced, separated or still married) were interviewed again. The study revealed that two-thirds of the unhappily married spouses who remained together were actually happier five years later. The opposite was true for those divorced. Although divorce was a temporary escape from pain, it introduced new emotional and psychological difficulties. In a nutshell, unless problems are severe and/or life threatening, weather the storm—it's well worth it.

Who we are when single will be who we are when married, at least initially. For this reason, it's vitally important to develop qualities now that we'll want to continue to develop throughout marriage. Marriages that begin with right intentions but end in divorce often fail to continue to nurture and strengthen the relationship. Just as investing in physical exercise builds

> *Who we are when single will be who we are when married—at least initially.*

and strengthens the body, ongoing spiritual, emotional and other psychological investments build and strengthen relationships. In the fitness industry, for example, the majority of those who lose weight from dieting gain it back—they don't make an ongoing investment in a lifestyle that promotes health and fitness. *A temporary solution cannot solve a long-term problem.* Regardless if weight is lost through dieting or pills, if the core of the problem is not addressed, success is difficult to maintain. In the same way, if we don't address thoughts, attitudes and behavioral patterns that hinder a successful relationship, long-term success may be difficult. I often advise clients that what it takes to lose weight, is what it takes to keep it off—the same is true in marriage—what it takes to develop and build the relationship is what it takes to keep it going!

> *What it takes to develop and build the relationship is what it takes to keep it going!*

I'm reminded of a popular saying . . . *a true measure of a person is not who they were, but who they will become.* One redeeming, yet largely unacknowledged fact of life, is that our past does not have to determine our present or our future! Yes, there are consequences to our actions, but past failures do not have to prevent future success. In fact, many successful people have replaced the concept of *failure* with a more positive

> *God wants us to move forward in forgiveness, rather than remain imprisoned by regret.*

concept of *feedback*. Don't misunderstand . . . if failure is related to sin, it's wrong, but God wants us to move forward in forgiveness, rather than remain imprisoned by regret.

THE MOST IMPORTANT DECISION

It is difficult to share my past, but I do so with the hope that I can help others avoid failed relationships.

Although I was a successful corporate executive, the years during my late twenties were the worst years of my life. I was driven, but for the wrong reasons. I felt a sense of purpose, but it left me feeling empty. I was passionate, but for the wrong things. As a result of my misguided focus, my life took several unnecessary turns for the worse—including my wife of four years filing for divorce. I quickly learned that before meaningful, lasting change can occur on the outside, it first must occur on the inside. We cannot successfully change actions and/or circumstances without first changing the inner condition of our heart—we must *choose to change from the inside out.*

For years, I focused on everything society had to offer, but I ultimately found that it offered little of lasting value or satisfaction. Desperate for direction and fulfillment, I began to search the pages of a Bible shelved long ago with other memorabilia from my past. As I read, two Scriptures seemed to leap from the pages: "For what profit is it to a man if he gains the whole world, and is himself destroyed or lost?" (Luke 9:25), and ". . . Today, if you will hear His voice, do not harden your hearts" (Hebrews 4:7). I realized that I had been looking for fulfillment in all the wrong places. While I had focused on externals, such as prosperity, physical fitness and relationships, I had starved my spirit. I had been independent, self-centered and prideful—I had hardened my heart.

Within the months that followed, my passion and my purpose for life became clearer than ever once I recommitted my life to Christ. And direction? Well, direction was uncertain. However, I was now open for wherever His lead might take me. Little did I know that I would soon walk away from a lucrative career and face the unknown to begin writing the *WHAT WORKS Book Series*, and to develop a health and weight-loss website based on principles often overlooked within our culture.

It was a time of financial uncertainty, but very clear spiritual certainty. Psalm 32:8 helped to ease my mind, "I will instruct you and teach you in the way you should go; I will guide you with My eye." I may not have known where my steps were leading, but God did.

We're living in times of great uncertainty for our country, but there is tremendous comfort, direction and strength in adhering to spiritual principles that have guided mankind consistently throughout the centuries. The basis for success in any area of life is founded on spiritual truths. Many are searching for spiritual direction and fulfillment, and that is why it's essential that we address this issue first.

"Religion" comes with many faces. New Age and other religions are popular, and have been throughout time, because people have a deep desire to connect spiritually—God created us for that purpose. *Searching for spiritual fulfillment isn't wrong, but where we search can be.*

On the eve of writing this chapter, I was returning from a women's conference in Central California where I spoke on the subject of health, fitness and weight-loss. I was amazed to see how many of the speakers focused on spirituality and "finding one's inner-self", but none mentioned a personal relationship with Jesus Christ. I asked one of the speakers if her material was biblically based. She said that she believed in a higher power, and that her information drew from Buddhism, New Age and Scripture.

There is tremendous power and wisdom in the Bible; even worldly scholars recognize its influence. Most major religions take portions from the Bible, but we can't take from the Bible what we choose and disregard the rest. I liken it to someone skimming through the pages of *WHAT WORKS When "Diets" Don't,* and reading: *eat whatever you choose.* In it's entirety it actually reads, "If you follow these guidelines, stay within these ranges and avoid these foods, you can eat whatever foods you choose." Reading and following only chosen portions of information can mean failure, not success. *Owning a Bible doesn't lead to spiritual health any more than owning a treadmill leads to physical health. If we apply only what we choose, we can easily miss what we need.*

TODAY'S DECISION, TOMORROW'S DESTINY

The first principle, *choosing to change from the inside out*, is the most crucial to healthy relationships but also the most ignored. In

> *Before lasting change occurs on the outside, it first must occur on the inside.*

order for change to occur on the outside, it must first occur on the inside. For instance, I had to accept the fact that I was a sinner who needed a Savior before I could truly change from the inside out. I stopped blaming people, places or things, and started taking responsibility for my actions from an inward position, and began moving in a positive direction.

Turning Point Ministries describes four emotional states that can prevent change. The first is *blame* (feeds denial). Second is *resentment* (anger at the situation). Third is *rationalization* (making excuses for actions). The final state is *hopelessness* (the result of a perceived helpless condition). Many people fail to move forward because they are trapped within these stages and hindered by their emotional state. They must come to resolve, or release these attitudes before they can move forward. Without an

> *Choosing today changes tomorrow!*

inward change (thoughts), an outward change (actions) is unlikely. Choosing to change your lifestyle from the inside out begins with a choice. Choosing today changes tomorrow!

You may be saying, "What does all this have to do with being single or building solid relationships?" My friend, it has everything to do with being single and strengthening relationships. Without Jesus Christ truly leading the way, all efforts will be in vain. It's been said that *sin takes us farther than we want to go, costs us more than we want to pay and keeps us longer than we want to stay.* I couldn't agree more. Many singles go through life entering new relationships with past baggage, or old issues. Accepting a new life in Christ can change that. II Corinthians 5:17 states: "Therefore, if anyone is in Christ, he is a new creation; old things have passed away; behold, all things have become new." *Your past is forgiven, your present secure and your future certain;* through Christ you are a brand new person. Though much of our past may remain in our thought life, we can overcome by replacing negative thoughts with Scriptures.

Jesus has made Himself available to us. He gave us the ability to think, to reason and to choose to accept Him or reject Him. I believe that life is an intentional act; it is not the result of a random, cosmic explosion that unexplainably organized itself into magnificent beauty, intelligence and the ability to love. It takes more faith to believe that we are here because chaos randomly organized itself rather than by a deliberate act of a Creator.

God did not create without a purpose. If life is a gift, there's a Giver. If we were created, there's a Creator. If there is a master plan, there's a Master Planner. With this understanding, it would be a waste of precious time not to allow God to direct our lives.

If you're reading this and are skeptical because of past experiences with religion, that's ok; religion is not the answer— *a relationship with Christ* is. There is a clear difference.

➢ Religion says, "I have to follow rules." A relationship with Christ says, "I want to follow His plan for my life."

➢ Religion says, "I have to go to church." A relationship with Christ says, "I want to position myself to learn more, worship Him and benefit from fellowship."

➢ Religion offers a set of rituals; a relationship with Jesus offers unfailing guidance.

➢ Religion is man's attempt to find God; relationship assures us of His presence.

I believe that many "Christian" marriages fail because they confuse "religion" with a true relationship with Christ (the solid foundation for relationships with others). Married couples may know Scripture but, often, they do not apply Scripture to the act of maintaining the relationship.

I'm frequently amazed at the number of people who no longer attend church simply because of a bad experience, dislike of the music or some similar reason. Can you imagine if we applied that thought to everyday living? If we have a bad experience at a restaurant, should we never dine out again? If we have a bad experience at a health club, should we never exercise again? If we have a bad experience with our vehicle, should we never drive again? This rationale doesn't make sense. However, I clearly understand that there are some churches that should be avoided. The key is to compare what they're saying and doing with the Word of God—look also for characteristics such as acceptance, encouragement, love and support.

We have faith in banks, businesses, vehicles, buildings and friends, but when it comes to having faith in an all knowing, all-powerful God, many have trouble. They have difficulty accepting Jesus as God in human form, or they believe that He is close to a fairytale. They don't understand why God sent His Son, if they believe at all. Working closely with my father helped me better understand this truth. Many times, as a teen, I assisted him throughout the day. He owned a construction company that specialized in the installation of underground services. At times, I would jump into a five, six or seven foot deep trench to install a new pipeline. Five minutes into the installation, it was sometimes obvious that I was at a loss. From above, my dad gave helpful directives like, "Do it this way", or "Don't do it like that, you'll break the pipe." After many attempts to help from his position above, he would inevitably jump down into the trench and show me how to do my job successfully. It wasn't until he came down to my level, demonstrated the proper technique and explained the process that I fully understood. And sometimes, he would simply have to do it for me. Although not perfect, I made vast improvements as the training sessions continued. In the same way, Jesus was sent to teach us how to lead godly, meaningful lives and to "save us from ourselves". In essence, the price was so great for the damage done left to ourselves, that at the end of His

PRINCIPLE ONE:

CHOOSING TO CHANGE FROM THE INSIDE OUT

ministry, Jesus paid the highest price of all by dying to redeem us from our sins.

Make no mistake about it, the greatest commitment that you will ever make is to develop and guard your spiritual health. *If you're searching but not finding, hurting and not healing and living but not loving, I encourage you to first look to the One who has the answers and commit your life to Him.*

No matter what you've done or have been through, you have the ability and availability to accept or return to Jesus and become as new. Again, a true measure of a person is not who they were, but who they will become.

> *A true measure of a person is not who they were, but who they will become.*

For those who have already made a decision to follow Christ, choosing to change simply means choosing to do what is right instead of choosing what is popular, or what feels good; sometimes, but not always, they are one and the same. Obeying God's Word affects everyone around you, including the one you choose to spend the rest of your life with. Far too many who accept Christ as their personal Savior leave it at that. They want eternal salvation but still want to be accepted by society. *Accepting Christ isn't the finish line; it's the starting point.* If you fall under this heading, I encourage you to seriously re-consider your commitment, realizing that one cannot serve both Christ and the world. It took me nearly seventeen years to realize that His laws are there to protect us, not to prevent us from enjoying life.

Before I recommitted my life, I went late to church on the days I attended and left as soon as the message was over. On weekends, I often drank, focused on making money and ignored the Christian faith I professed. It was sobering to read in Matthew 7:22, for the first time with open eyes, "Many will say to Me in that day, 'Lord, Lord have we not prophesied in Your name, cast out demons in Your name, and done many wonders in Your name?'" And He will say *". . . I never knew you; depart from Me, you who practice lawlessness"* (7:23—italics mine). Some might say that they don't understand how Jesus can say, "I never knew you." He's not denying their existence; He's denying a personal relationship with them. It became very clear when I applied it to my life, "But Lord, Lord . . . I attended church on the days that I didn't play golf, or go to the gym, or sleep in. I was a good person, and I helped others when I could." The answer was the same, "I never knew you; depart from Me." As an example, I can watch the Dodgers baseball games, read the players biographies and study their stats, but if I were to meet any of them, they would say, "I don't know you." *Knowing about someone is not knowing someone.* A close relationship is built through mutual commitment, servitude and spending time with a person. Christ has designed the way to develop a relationship with Him: read and obey His Word, and pray and seek His will for your life. I've been on both sides of the fence—there's no comparison.

Many go from relationship to relationship searching for someone to fill a need. As a result, their lives often become a roller coaster ride of emotions simply because they don't look to Jesus as their primary source of fulfillment. By placing Him first, all other relationships profit.

By placing Him first, all other relationships profit.

Just because the choice is made to acknowledge Him first, does not mean that life is easy. There is a constant battle within our minds. Galatians 5:17 (NLT) presents this fact: ". . . the Spirit gives us desires that are opposite from what the sinful nature desires. These two forces are constantly fighting each other, and your choices are never free from this conflict." In other words, our sinful nature and our nature in Christ are constantly at battle. A story, *The Battle Within,* taken from my first book illustrates this point:

The Battle Within

There was a young man who was determined to find help for his troubled life. After years of frustration and regret, he was deeply discouraged and despondent. He needed solid direction. He had worked several years and had nothing to show for it. He had been easily influenced, and most of his friends were major contributors to his negative attitude. As a result, his mind was constantly filled with depressing thoughts.

The young man was determined to find help. He walked to a neighboring church and found a pastor at work in his study. He told the pastor that he was a Christian but that he had a difficult life. He wanted to make better choices, but he couldn't seem to stay on track.

The young man continued, "It's as if I have two dogs constantly battling within me. One dog is evil and negative, while the other is good and positive!" He continued to say that the battles were long and very difficult; they drained him emotionally and mentally to the point of exhaustion. He explained further that he couldn't seem to make the right choices in life.

Without a moment's thought, the pastor asked the young man, "Which dog wins the battle?" Looking a bit confused, the young man said, "The constant struggle leaves me depressed and in a negative state. Isn't it obvious that the evil dog wins?" The pastor looked knowingly at the young man and wisely said, *"Then that's the dog you feed the most! If you want to experience victory, you need to starve that dog to death!"*

He realized, as should we, that the source of our strength comes from the food we choose—*what we feed grows, and what grows becomes the dominating force within our lives.*

> *The source of our strength comes from the food we choose.*

We need to be very selective in what we watch and listen to. Why would we willingly walk into the enemy's camp? Why would we feed wrong desires and thoughts? Feeding the flesh does nothing but bring war against the spirit. Proverbs 23:7 also reminds us that, ". . . as he thinks in his heart, so is he . . ." What we think provides the framework for who we become. Our thoughts become words, our words actions, our actions habits and our habits form our character

> *Our thoughts become words, our words actions, our actions habits and our habits form our character.*

(paraphrased motto of the Metropolitan Milwaukee YMCA). "For we are not fighting against people made of flesh and blood, but against the evil rulers and authorities of the unseen world, against those mighty powers of darkness who rule this world, and against

wicked spirits in the heavenly realms" (Ephesians 6:12 NLT).
Make no mistake about it, our greatest battle is within.

I once misunderstood those who chose not to watch certain
movies and television programs, attend certain events or listen to
suggestive secular music. I now
realize that *if I don't control my*
desires, my desires will control me—
right thinking creates right doing! For
instance, after I recommitted my life
to Christ, my cravings for alcohol seemed to increase at times. A
week or two would go by and eventually the desire to drink again
resurfaced. As I continued to analyze my situation, I noticed that
every time I watched certain television programs, listened to most
secular music or associated with the wrong crowd (a major snare),
the desire to drink would increase. I quickly learned that what we
feed grows and what grows becomes the controlling force within
our lives. If we want to experience a healthy and fulfilling life, we
must choose our food wisely. We'll never be completely free from
wrong desires; there is a constant struggle to resist temptation, but
there's a clear difference between a struggle and a lifestyle. Even
Christ was tempted, but he was not drawn away by sin.

> *Right thinking creates*
> *right doing.*

To recap, one of the primary ways to win the battle in our mind
is to feed it with the right information, and to be careful not to
walk willingly into the enemy's camp. Joyce Meyer has written an
exceptional book entitled: *Battlefield of the MIND*. I highly
recommend it for those wanting additional help in this area.

Perhaps you're still questioning what this has to do with
building relationships. It has everything to do with the process.
Remember, it is important to build
a strong foundation that will
support lasting relationships.
If the foundation is weak, the
structure is not sound.

> *If the foundation is*
> *weak, the structure*
> *is not sound.*

Principle one, *choosing to change from the inside out*, whether accepting Christ for the first time, or re-committing to Him wholeheartedly, is the most important step to take. Change your life and it will change you.

> *Change your life and it will change you.*

BLESSINGS JUST AROUND THE CORNER

While single, focus on building your life on solid character traits and recognize that who you are as a single will be who you are when married. People do change after marriage, but most bring with them traits and habits from single life. What will this mean for you or your future spouse? With this in mind, focus on changing counterproductive habits that will hinder a successful marriage. We don't get in life what we want but rather what we are. If one desires a committed, honest spouse, one should develop those same qualities to attract that type of individual.

> *If one desires a committed, honest spouse, one should develop those same qualities to attract that type of individual.*

Another aspect of *choosing to change from the inside out*, at least for me, was patience. Patience, patience, patience! I often spent my time looking for someone to date, and I'd frequently attend church for the wrong reasons. I finally realized that certain areas in my life needed improvement. Why would God bring a blessing into my life before I was ready to be a blessing in return? I prayed David's prayer from Psalm 51:10, "Create in me a clean heart, O God, and renew a steadfast spirit within me." I added, "I will follow You wholeheartedly, and when I'm ready, that door will open." I thought that it would take a few weeks, maybe even a few months, but after six months of waiting, I began to lose hope. I continued to say the same prayer, followed His lead and worked on my character. After nearly a year of waiting and a total of three years living a single life, I felt that I was ready. I said Lord, "You bring her to me; I don't want to be out of Your will."

A few weeks later, I attended a new Sunday night service for young adults and thought I'd meet someone for sure. When I arrived, my focus was on finding someone when it should have been on personal growth. Needless to say, I didn't meet anyone. I thought, "Well, maybe next Sunday." And again, I didn't meet anyone. I followed this pattern for nearly two months, until one Sunday, during praise and worship, I realized that I was still there for the wrong reason. I prayed, "Lord, I'm here for you. Even if I never meet anyone, I want to know You better." Something broke in me. I attended the next several Sundays and was not interested in meeting anyone; I was there to develop a relationship with the Lord, and it truly felt good.

Following another evening service a month later, I saw a girl who I had dinner with a year and a half prior but nothing had sparked then. It may have been that God said, "Here is your gift, but it's up to you if and when you receive it."

A year and a half had changed us both. She had grown strong spiritually and I was re-visiting my feelings about her. Our relationship eventually grew into desire for a lasting commitment. I often smile to think that what I had been looking for throughout Southern California was actually two blocks away. (Many times, if we slow down and wait, our blessings are just around the corner.) God has promised that if you will seek Him first with right motives and commit your ways to Him, He will direct you (Proverbs 3:6 paraphrased).

The months that followed were not easy; we focused on avoiding physical intimacy and we waited on the Lord for timing and direction. Additionally, I hadn't been involved in a serious relationship in years and the "ghost of marriage past" was haunting me. As a result, fear and issues with trust entered the new relationship—the enemy often resurrects past failures to prevent future success. Divorce is devastating; it not only affects your life for years to come, it severely affects those closest to you. Had it not been for Morgan's

> *The enemy often resurrects past failures to prevent future success.*

love, patience and understanding, I doubt we would have married. What the enemy used for evil by trying to confuse and depress me, God ultimately used for good. Her kindness and commitment began to calm my fears.

On a closing note, as I prayed and waited for a potential spouse, one Scripture encouraged me time and time again, and it may encourage you. Paul writes in 1 Corinthians 7:17 (NLT), "You must accept whatever situation the Lord has put you in, and continue on as you were when God first called you . . ." When married couples made reference to this quote, I'd think, "That's easy for you to say, you're married." Nevertheless, the Scripture helped me to realize that *no matter what state I was in relationally, I could also be in the center of God's will.* That thought was my buffer against on-going discouragement.

Changing Direction

Choosing to change is the first step and the most important. As you begin, remember that a strong foundation will cost something, but a weak foundation can cost more. If you are choosing to accept Christ as your personal Savior for the first time, continue to build on solid ground. Psalm 11:3 states, "If the foundations are destroyed, what can the righteous do?" and Isaiah 7:9 states, ". . . if you do not stand firm in your faith, you will not stand at all" (NIV). These Scriptures are to encourage and to illustrate the importance of continually building your faith on God's Word. Strengthen your foundation . . .

1. Find a Bible based, Christ-centered church.

2. Devote a portion of your day to prayer.

3. Purchase a good study Bible; read and journal.

4. Memorize Scriptures and use them as a standard for direction and decision.

5. Develop relationships with those who will encourage you to grow in your faith.

QUESTIONS TO CONSIDER:

"Who you are when single will be who you are when married, at least initially.*"* What will you bring into the relationship? Where can you improve?

Are you focused on finding the right person or being the right person?

Consider the principle of sowing and reaping. What are you sowing in the lives of others? What will you reap?

Love doesn't leave people—people leave love. How will you strengthen yourself in this area?

What do you believe holds marriage together through the difficult times?

Do you believe in forgiveness regardless of the circumstance?

Do you generally do what is right or what is popular?

Who and/or what in your life tends to hinder personal growth?

Change requires that we be willing. Check your attitude concerning the following and comment: *denial, unforgiveness, rationalization,* and *hopelessness.*

Memorize Romans 12:2, "And do not be conformed to this world, but be transformed by the renewing of your mind, that you may prove what is that good and acceptable and perfect will of God."

Knowledge plus wisdom equals results. One without the other is like a ship without a course—without both, it's difficult to reach your destination.

CHAPTER TWO

2

Principle

Acquire Knowledge—
Apply Wisdom

Minimize the damage—use the right tool

Many of my teen years and early twenties were spent working
for our family business. One morning while I was digging a
trench with a backhoe, I broke an existing water line. Within
minutes, the trench filled with water. I rushed to shut off the valve
but the handle appeared broken. I struggled to close it with a
screwdriver, a pair of pliers and other wrenching tools, but
nothing worked. Hesitantly, I called my dad to tell him that I
couldn't stop hundreds of gallons of water from pouring into the
street. When he arrived, clearly frustrated, he reached into his
truck and grabbed a long pole with a special socket attached. As
he placed the socket on the "broken valve" and turned it, the
water stopped immediately. He reminded me, not so patiently, of

his words just weeks prior. He had instructed me to keep the special wrench with me at all times for emergencies like this.

I learned two important lessons. First, I received proper instruction, but I failed to listen to my father's advice. Had I used the right tool, the damage, if any, would have been minimal. In the same way, biblical principles and godly wisdom are available to us, but it's our choice whether we use them or not. I thought I had other options, the pliers, screwdriver and other tools seemed as if they would work; I felt I could manage without the water-meter wrench, but my failure to heed my father's advice cost us the price of the job. In the same way, we often think of "our way" as best and God's principles as optional when, in fact, the opposite is true: God's directives are essential and absolute.

Second, I realized that I could not fix the problem alone and called for my father's help. Likewise, we all encounter problems, and need to ask for help even when

He should be the first resort, not the last.

problems are self-created. Calling on our Heavenly Father should be the first resort, not the last. Had I called my father first—or listened initially—the damage would have been considerably less. In the same way, heed the *right* advice and look to the *right* source for help in building a foundation of wisdom in your life.

GAUGING GOOD JUDGMENT—CONSIDER THE RESULTS

One way to gauge wisdom, or good judgment, is to consider the results. In Matthew 11:19, the Jewish people were having difficulty grasping the unexpected nature of Jesus' ministry. Many alleged that John the Baptist, the one chosen to prepare the way for Jesus, was demon-possessed and that Jesus was a glutton and drunkard. Instead of arguing with them, Jesus made this statement ". . . But wisdom is shown to be right by what results from it" (NLT). In other words, godly wisdom bears righteous fruit. People received healing and deliverance, and many accepted Christ as their Savior. This was obviously not the work of demons, drunkards or gluttons. Jesus encouraged them to look at the end result and not at how things appeared.

Again, we gauge good judgment by considering its results. If single, are your choices producing the results you want? If dating, is the relationship heading in the right direction? If not, consider who's leading you—God's Word or the cultural value system. Does our present society promote good judgment and/or produce good outcomes? Is society building healthy families, mentoring children and developing admirable character? What are the results of today's relative value system and disregard for God's absolutes?

Today's value system promotes pro-choice and de-values the unborn child.

What is the result?

> ➤ Approximately 1.4 million babies are aborted each year in the U.S. If the names of all the children who have been terminated since 1970 were placed on a monument, much like that of the Vietnam Memorial Wall, the wall would span over 50 miles.

In the early 1960's, the Supreme Court held that prayer and God's Word had no place in the public school system, and safe sex has been the focus of sex education.

What is the result?

> ➤ Each day over 2,700 teens become pregnant.

> ➤ Premarital sex among 15-year-old students has increased almost 1,000 percent since 1962.

> ➤ Over three million teens become infected each year with an STD.

> ➤ Incredibly, talking, chewing gum and making noise were the top three public school problems in the early sixties. Currently, rape, robbery and assault lead the list, followed by burglary, arson, bombings, murder and suicide.

Society promotes money, fame and personal assets as the primary measures of success.

What is the result?

> ➤ America leads the way in fatherless homes and broken families. Numbers rise as men and women continue to measure success by what they accomplish in the workplace rather than by what they accomplish at home.

Society encourages the consumption of "junk" food. Athletes promote it, parents purchase it and kids enjoy it.

<u>What is the result?</u>

➢ Poor nutrition is killing more Americans than any other health factor, and well over half of the adults in America are obese as a result.

➢ One third of the teens in California are overweight or at risk of it. This can lead to diabetes, cancer and heart disease as teens become adults.

➢ Currently, cancer affects one in three people and is often associated with poor nutrition.

➢ In the last sixty years, diabetes has increased 600 percent to 1,000 percent.

Society's wisdom promotes pornography as a harmless expression of freedom of speech.

<u>What is the result?</u>

➢ Teens and adults are becoming addicted to pornography at alarming rates.

➢ Pornography is considered a matter of free speech, while God's Word is banned in public schools and other arenas within our communities.

➢ Pornography is often a major influence in the lives of those who commit sex crimes.

So much for the fruit of a relative value system and disregard for absolute truths; is this the direction that we want to go—that you want to go? If not, make a change. Granted, it's disheartening to read statistics like these, but knowledge is power. What does this have to do with being single? Everything! Restoration is possible as we follow God's commands, seek direction and pursue the opportunity that God has given us to make an impact within our families. *Be grateful and consider it a privilege that God has chosen you for such a time as this.*

THE TOP THREE THINGS TO AVOID

You were created for a reason. Your life has purpose. No matter what you've gone through or are going through, there is a purpose and a destiny for your life. According to 1 John 2:16 (paraphrased), the enemy uses three methods to abort success . . . the *lust of the flesh* (what we crave), the *lust of the eyes* (what is pleasing to the eye) and the *pride of life* (arrogance).

The lust of the flesh. Lust can be defined as desire over the boundary lines. All of us struggle with lust in some form or another, the question is do we entertain the thought until it fuels desire, or do we walk away? Desire is not wrong, but what we do with it can be. If our hearts are sincere and teachable, God can bless us, but if we purposely

> *Desire is not wrong, but what we do with it can be.*

engage in sin, we remove His protection. *Being tempted isn't sin—surrendering to it is.* God is merciful to forgive and bestow blessings as we repent and make necessary lifestyle changes. Feelings of lust can be overcome as we read His Word, protect our eyes and ears, educate ourselves, apply wisdom and surround ourselves with those who lift us up rather than pull us down.

As a final word of encouragement, God will not allow us to be tempted beyond what we are able. 1 Corinthians 10:13 states, ". . . God is faithful, who will not allow you to be tempted beyond what you are able, but with the temptation will also make the

> *The door of temptation swings both ways—you can enter or exit.*

way of escape, that you may be able to bear it." The door of temptation swings both ways—you can enter or exit.

The lust of the eyes can be defined as coveting, or desiring something such as a trophy wife or husband, expensive home or vehicle. Being drawn by attraction, depending on the situation, is not wrong as long as the motive for the relationship isn't based solely on looks. For instance, although I was greatly attracted to my wife's physical beauty, it was her character that held me. When attraction is based on inner qualities, appeal can last forever. Beauty fades and it is important to value the person beneath. As you move forward in a relationship, frequently evaluate your motives for pursuing. Are you intrigued with beauty, so much so that serious character flaws are overlooked? If so, rethink the relationship.

The pride of life is the opposite of humility. It can be defined as conceit, or a sense of superiority in who we are or what we posses. Proverbs 6:16-17 says, ". . . the Lord hates a proud look . . ." Self-centeredness is closely related to pride. When we believe that our needs are more important than the needs of others, and we think more highly of ourselves than we should, pride is a problem and it will severely hinder a relationship. Pride of life causes us to place more emphasis on things than on people. A popular saying bears consideration—*God intended that we love people and use things; instead we tend to love things and use people.* Pride causes us to take pleasure in the things of the world rather than the things of God. Husbands and wives don't marry filled with love and passion one day only to lose it the next. Marriage slowly deteriorates through more attention to self than spouse. Most who are divorced will say that their marriage was initially good, but with time, one or both stopped loving—largely because of selfishness. As a word of encouragement, according to *The Book of Romance* (Thomas Nelson, Inc.), only 1 out of 1,050 marriages in which the husband and wife read the Bible together daily, end in divorce.

> *Only 1 out of 1,050 marriages in which the husband and wife read the Bible together daily, end in divorce.*

GUARD YOUR HEART AND IT WILL GUARD YOU

Principle two, *acquire knowledge—apply wisdom,* is extremely important when dating. Be careful to whom you give your heart. Emotions can easily cause you to give your heart away with little thought. Emotions are merely a dance to the music of the heart and the dance can change with the music—not a very stable resource for making sound decisions.

Our heart regulates emotions, and emotions often control actions. Proverbs 4:23 (NLT) states, "Above all else, guard your heart, for it affects everything you do." Samson, an Old Testament character known for his strength, demonstrates the effects of giving one's heart away to the wrong person.

Samson was a Nazarite who was dedicated to the Lord at birth. The Lord blessed him as he grew and gave him extraordinary strength when he

PRINCIPLE TWO:
ACQUIRE KNOWLEDGE—
APPLY WISDOM

fought against his enemy, the Philistines. Eventually, Samson fell in love with a woman named Delilah. He confided in her and told her the source of his strength. Judges 16:16–17 (KJV) states, "And it came to pass, when she pressed him daily with her words, and urged him . . . that he told her all his heart, and said unto her, 'There hath not come a rasor upon mine head . . . if I be shaven, then my strength will go from me, and I shall become weak, and be like any other man.'"

The Philistines hated Samson and paid Delilah to trap him. When she discovered the source of his strength, she reported it to the Philistines and they took him captive. Samson failed to guard his heart, and thus, lost his strength and power, and was overthrown by the enemy. In the same way, relationships are weakened when the heart is given too early or to the wrong person. Simply stated, guard your heart and it will guard you!

Guard your heart and it will guard you!

God did redeem Samson. He was able to regain his strength long enough to again defeat his enemy, but it also cost him his life.

Few things can hinder our lives more than misplaced emotions. When we are happy and positive, everything seems to go well, but when we're down and have a negative attitude, it's difficult to find the motivation to see things through. Our enemy does not want a well-guarded heart; he wants us exposed and vulnerable. He also wants us so emotionally scarred from past relationships that we spend years trying to rebuild and restore broken lives. Again, Scripture states: *"Above all else, guard your heart . . ."* Guarding your heart should be a priority, not a consideration.

To guard means to raise a protective barrier and shield our emotions. One of the best ways to guard the heart is to use both wisdom and knowledge. The Hebrew word for heart is *mind;* guarding your heart literally means guarding your mind. In short, be careful who and what you listen to, what you tell yourself and who you allow to influence you.

> *Knowledge is knowing what to do; wisdom is doing what you know.*

Knowledge is knowing what to do; wisdom is doing what you know. For example, many know that pre-marital sex is wrong, but those who actually abstain are using both knowledge and wisdom. Many want to do what is right, but living a life of moral excellence is challenging. One can make a mental decision to abstain, but still fail.

Guard your heart while dating and/or courting:

1. Don't allow yourself to be in a compromising position that may weaken your defense.

2. When possible, date in the company of friends or family.

3. Share time together at public events.

4. Avoid discussing future plans such as marriage or children, too soon.

5. Don't rush the relationship; allow it to grow at a healthy pace.

6. Don't become emotionally attached—keep your other interests alive.

7. Avoid making decisions based solely on emotion.

8. Take two or three days a week away from the relationship. Allow time to think, and seek God's will for the relationship.

9. Guard your speech. Don't say things that may stimulate premature desires.

Listen and Learn As You Guard

An inner voice often directs our decisions throughout the day; the best way to guard the heart is to follow the correct leading. Dr. Don Rannikar's book, *Choosing God's Best,* outlines eight ways to listen correctly.

The correct leading . . .	**The incorrect leading . . .**
Stills you	Rushes you
Leads you	Pushes you
Reassures you	Frightens you
Enlightens you	Confuses you
Encourages you	Discourages you
Comforts you	Worries you
Calms you	Obsesses you
Convicts you	Condemns you

Once we give our lives to Christ and seek His direction, we can sense His lead, but if we're actively engaging in sin, His direction will be hard to distinguish, if at all. Hearing God's voice can keep us from sin, or sin can keep us from hearing God's voice.

> *Hearing God's voice can keep us from sin, or sin can keep us from hearing God's voice.*

You can hear the still, small voice of the Holy Spirit by spending time in prayer and learning from God's Word. Stop, listen and learn. If you've ever sat quietly outside your home in the calm of the morning, you've probably noticed many of the sounds that you do not hear throughout the day. Those sounds generally continue throughout the day, but as the day progresses, they are overcome by the sounds of our busy lives. In order to hear, it's necessary to remove oneself from the activity of the day. When God spoke to Elijah in 1 Kings 19:11–12, the Scriptures state that the wind and the fire came, and that the storms thundered, but that God was not in them; He was, however, in the still, small voice that followed (paraphrased). God wants our undivided attention each and every day.

Avoid this checklist when dating or courting

➤ RUSHING OR RESPONDING TO A SENSE OF URGENCY

➤ OBSESSION

➤ CONFUSION

Responding to a Sense of Urgency

Without a shadow of doubt, moving too quickly can have major consequences. When dating or courting, for example, we often want answers and we want them now. It's difficult to patiently wait; we've been waiting! In analyzing failed relationships, *many couples will say, "We moved too quickly"; rarely will you hear, "We moved too slowly."*

Patience may be compared to a control valve used to help us avoid making decisions based on emotional response. Much like a control device used for a dam to release water, if the valve is broken, water levels rise and can overflow, causing destruction below. In the same way, if we don't allow patience to control our feelings, they may build to unhealthy levels and cause damage.

Patience can either strengthen a couple's relationship or help them part on good terms. If the relationship is breeding obsession, focusing unhealthy thoughts, energy and efforts on the other person, it's time to back away. One can never go wrong by saying, "God, I believe that I moved too fast and haven't been patient in this relationship, I want to take time away and focus on You. I trust that You will lead me and show me what to do."

If you feel rushed, simply step back and re-evaluate. Stepping back doesn't mean ending the relationship; it means patiently seeking God's direction as you move forward. This also provides an opportunity to see how the other person handles the challenge. Are they patient and supportive or do they question your decision to patiently wait? If they question it, their motive for pursuing the relationship may differ from yours.

Obsession

Obsession is often defined as a fixation, fascination or a passion. It can move us from the realm of self-control into self-destruction. We are more likely to compromise our standards when we become obsessed with a thought or a person. The need for relationship isn't wrong, but how we fulfill it can be.

The need for relationship isn't wrong, but how we fulfill it can be.

Obsession is powerful and can be a form of idolatry (placing something or someone above God). If not managed, obsession can consume our lives. For example, a couple may begin seeing each other two or three days a week. Three days then becomes four, four becomes six, and so on until their entire lives are consumed by each other. Focus on moderation and realistic expectations as you move forward.

CONFUSION

Confusion can be defined as perplexing and uncertain thoughts, and can feed anxiety. Anxiety can occur when the relationship reaches unhealthy levels. It can cause worry and unwarranted stress. When we are impatient and obsessed, we can easily become confused; confusion often leads to emotional, unsound decisions. We may say and do things that jeopardize the relationship when the foundation of trust is being established. How many relationships may have worked, or ended with less pain, if only the couple had patiently waited for God's timing. It's been said that the right thing at the wrong time is the wrong thing. Patience allows you time to see the relationship for what it really is, to see each other in a variety of situations and under a variety of conditions. Waiting provides opportunity to determine if this is the person that you could spend a lifetime with. Again, we rarely, if ever, hear people say, "I waited too long", but we do hear "I moved too fast". Simply slow down . . . it's worth the wait.

> *The right thing at the wrong time is the wrong thing.*

Be Open for Feedback

Love is not only impatient at times, but blind as well. Seek feedback from those you trust. Invite them to share their thoughts about the relationship from their perspective; this can be a tremendous help. Proverbs 15:22 states, "Plans go wrong for lack of advice; many counselors bring success" (NLT). Those counseling can generally offer advice and make distinctions based on objective observations rather than emotions as we might be inclined to do. Be careful. From time to time, you might be tempted to find someone to confirm your feelings—asking parents, co-workers or friends for advice until you hear what you *want* to hear and not necessarily what you *need* to hear.

Don't exaggerate your partner's positive character traits while neglecting character flaws to gain approval. *If the truth has to be altered to make the relationship appear better than it is, reconsider the relationship.* When we are honest and open, others can make an accurate assessment of the

> *Integrity guides better than others can.*

relationship. Proverbs 11:3 was a tremendous help to me: "The integrity of the upright will guide them . . ." Seek godly counsel, be patient, use wisdom and live a morally upright life, while allowing integrity to guide you.

All Too Common

When Rob and Susan discussed their relationship with close friends and family, they presented their partner as flawless. Rob neglected to mention Susan's serious struggle with bitterness, pride and self-centeredness, while Susan neglected to disclose Rob's weekend binges with alcohol and his inappropriate, flirtatious attitude toward other women.

Both Susan and Rob attended church from time to time. They rarely, if ever, opened their Bible, yet they described the other person as a committed Christian. Thus, their friends and family supported the relationship. In reality, they had serious issues that needed attention before a relationship could be considered.

Well into the relationship, encouraged by others who noticed warning signs, Rob and Susan sought pre-engagement counseling with Susan's pastor.

During the first few visits, they took personality tests and discussed the possibility of marriage. Again, they misrepresented themselves to the pastor, however the pastor sensed problems and questioned them. He recommended that they postpone a committed relationship and work on personal weaknesses. Displeased with the advice, a meeting with Rob's pastor was scheduled. This time when the pastor asked questions, they altered the truth so the pastor would support the relationship.

Rob and Susan both believed that they would change the other person once married. Unfortunately, their marriage lasted only eighteen months. Their lack of integrity and a firm foundation led to an affair and, ultimately, to divorce. Rob and Susan continually ignored wisdom and sound judgment and, like many, married only to divorce.

Does a contractor build a house without a set of plans? In the same way, how can we build healthy relationships without a blueprint? When we remove God's wisdom from the building process, we discard the instructions.

QUESTIONS TO CONSIDER:

Do you agree with the statement, "One way to gauge good judgment is to consider the results?" What are the results of important choices you've recently made? What changes, if any, need to be made?

How do wisdom and knowledge differ?

Hearing God's voice can keep us from sin, or sin can keep us from hearing God's voice. Do you agree?

Are there areas in which you feel rushed, obsessed or confused? If so, what can be done to change those feelings?

Are there any areas in your life where the truth is being altered to make the situation appear better than it is?

If you are currently in a relationship, what potential problems do you see? Do others see?

Memorize 1 John 2:16, "For all that is in the world, the lust of the flesh and the lust of the eyes and the boastful pride of life, is not from the Father, but is from the world" (updated NASB).

*Our strengths are seen in what
we stand for, our weaknesses
in what we fall for.*

CHAPTER THREE

Principle

The Pain of Discipline vs. the Pain of Regret

It's easier to pull down than to pull up

Think for a moment. If you are standing on a wall, is it easier to pull someone up to your level, or to be pulled down to theirs? Without much thought, you conclude that it's easier to be pulled down. Likewise, the downward pull of society is strong, especially when one is not firmly anchored.

The question of being *equally yoked* arises routinely during singles' conferences. Christian singles often look for reasons to date unbelievers. Consequently, the principle of the equal yoke is compromised and many find themselves out of balance under the weight of a challenging relationship. It's easy to believe that you'll convert the other person once you begin dating. Not so, often the unbeliever has the leverage. The Bible reminds us that we are greatly influenced by the company that we keep (I Corinthians 15:33). The pull of society is strong and it takes an enormous amount of energy to maintain an up-hill stride; an unequal yoke adds weight to the climb—we may enjoy the friendship but we can be wounded as easily by friendly fire as we can by a foe. More directly, God counsels us in II Corinthians 6:14, "Do not be unequally yoked together with unbelievers. For what fellowship has righteousness with lawlessness? And what communion has light with darkness?" Although this command is crystal clear, many read it with clouded vision. Some may claim to be Christians but that doesn't mean that they are walking in obedience to God's Word—look for the fruit that is produced by their lifestyle. Don't compromise. If they don't have the qualities you're looking for in a future spouse, don't lower your standards, keep them high. Many times, the problem isn't that we raise our standard and miss it, it's that we lower it and hit it.

> *We can be wounded as easily by friendly fire as we can by a foe.*

While talking to a group of young adults, our friend, Pastor David Sill, offered this advice . . . "Follow wholeheartedly after Christ and simply see who keeps up." Countless times in the Old Testament, God warned His people not to be unequally yoked with other nations, and countless times their disregard led to their downfall. *Who we associate with may be who we become;* we can be either pressed positively or depressed depending on their influence. An unequal yoke not only refers to marriage, it refers to close associates as well. I'm not suggesting that Christians only interact with other Christians; we are called to minister to others in all areas of life, but if the association is pulling us in the wrong direction, it's time to reconsider the relationship, or at least, establish boundaries.

> *"Follow wholeheartedly after Christ and simply see who keeps up."*

Love and passion are strong emotions—it feels so good, it must be right. Wrong! Do not base decisions on your emotions, base them on God's Word. Rather than struggling under the weight and pull of an unequal yoke, choose an equal yoke; it will increase strength, divide the weight and ease the journey.

CONTROL DESIRE BEFORE IT CONTROLS YOU

Many recognize the need for discipline but feel they don't have the strength of character to possess it, when in fact, they do. For instance, if it were possible to offer a million dollars to those who discontinue a harmful habit for one year, such as smoking or alcohol abuse, many would qualify for their reward at the end of the year. It's clear that they don't lack the capacity for discipline they lack motivation. The motivation of receiving the large sum of money would outweigh the desire to feed their habit. Isn't spiritual and physical health, and peace of mind far more valuable than money? Unfortunately, many continue in harmful addictions or sinful lifestyles even when physical and spiritual health are jeopardized.

Discipline is one of the most important character qualities we possess. Discipline and diligence are what allow us to control our desires rather than allowing our desires to control us. Ironically, those things we generally like to do such as viewing television, sleeping or surfing the Internet are easy, but working, reading the Bible, serving and spending quality time with family, seem to be the most difficult. That's why discipline is vitally important; it helps us do what we don't feel like doing, but later leaves us feeling deeply satisfied. Discipline is simply putting our choice into action. If we exercise discipline in one area, it will help to regulate and strengthen this control valve in other areas. For instance, those who regularly practice

> *Discipline is simply putting our choice into action.*

the discipline of exercising, often find that other areas of life improve. The principle of discipline cannot be overlooked when it comes to succeeding in any area of life as well, whether financially, relationally or spiritually. Be leery of those who say that discipline or willpower isn't important. Discipline is not only important to success—it's essential! Without a doubt, if we don't control our desires, our desires will often control us.

The pain of discipline often leads to fulfillment, pleasure and overall success. The pain of regret leads to disappointment, discouragement and frustration. In many cases, we can reverse the pain of regret, apply discipline and experience the great freedom that it brings. It's never too late! Are you working hard toward your goals, and are you working smart? Is what you're doing producing the results you want? If not, reconsider what you're doing and simply make another choice. Above all, make the change while you still have the choice and remember that the ability to "stick to it" is what separates those who succeed from those who almost succeed. You

> *The ability to "stick to it" is what separates those who succeed from those who almost succeed.*

possess tremendous inner power and strength. You've been given the power to make decisions, the power to develop habits and the power to choose at any given time. Many are willing to break a habit, lose weight, improve a marriage, attend church or seek God more fervently, but willingness alone is not enough. Willingness must be followed by action, and action, in this sense, is simply discipline in motion.

Forget past relational failures; instead decide what you're going to do with the days, weeks, months and years ahead. Don't live with ongoing regret. Take control of your life and change your direction. Don't look back unless it's the direction you want to go. You can't change where you've been, but you can change where you're going. The Apostle Paul stresses, ". . . but one thing I do, forgetting those things which are behind and reaching forward to those things which are ahead" (Philippians 3:13).

THREE KEYS TO SUCCESS

Now that we've discussed *choosing to change from the inside out, knowledge* and *discipline,* the first three principles, Psalm 1:1–3 provides three additional keys to success: "Blessed is the man who walks not in the counsel of the ungodly, nor stands in the path of sinners, nor sits in the seat of the scornful; but his delight is in the law of the Lord, and in His law he meditates day and night. He shall be like a tree planted by the rivers of water, that brings forth its fruit in its season, whose leaf also shall not wither; and whatever he does shall prosper."

I. *Blessed is the man who walks not in the counsel of the ungodly.* Who do you associate with, listen to or spend time with? Are they encouraging or discouraging you? What do you watch on TV and/or the Internet, or listen to on the radio? What do you read? Simply position yourself correctly to receive God's blessing.

II. *Do not stand in the path of the sinner or sit in the seat of the scornful.* If you're currently walking the path of sin, remove yourself, ask for forgiveness, repent and choose another path.

III. *Blessed are those who delight in and mediate day and night on the Word of God.* We make decisions daily, sometimes minute to minute. Meditating on God's Word helps us to solve problems based on sound principles. Daily Bible study provides the basis for decision-making, encouragement and wise counsel. Meditating on God's Word keeps His standard for living ever before us; it rewards us with stability and peace.

They who follow the keys to success . . . *will be like trees planted by water and will bear fruit in season; their leaves will not wither, and everything they do will prosper.* Bearing fruit in season means that some blessings are not always immediate. Figuratively speaking, you don't see a young apple tree bear abundant fruit; the tree would collapse under the weight. Likewise, God prepares and builds so we can hold the weight of His blessing. Can you envision the weight of responsibility that Billy Graham carried as he ministered to millions over his lifetime? He began faithfully in small things, and his ministry grew. Don't become frustrated if you haven't received what you've been waiting for; God is building and strengthening you. Remain firmly planted and allow God to add to your increase. Most of us will not minister to millions as Dr. Graham has done; however we are all capable of producing fruit within our daily lives by touching the lives of others, sometimes moment by moment.

PRINCIPLE THREE:

THE PAIN OF DISCIPLINE VS. THE PAIN OF REGRET

We are also told that *our leaves will not wither.* God brings life to our spirits and we are to be life giving. God sustains us so that we can help sustain others.

Verse three concludes . . . *and whatever he does will prosper.* Disciplining ourselves to avoid sin and ungodly counsel, combined with meditating and acting upon God's Word, will lead to a prosperous relationship with God, a prosperous marriage, a prosperous family, a prosperous career, a prosperous single life—all a reflection of a prosperous spirit.

SABOTAGING SUCCESS

I believe that a majority of marriages are failing because men are neglecting their God-given family responsibilities. In many cases, the actions of the husband determine the stability of the marriage. If a company fails, the president is held responsible. If a sports team fails, the coach is held responsible. If a marriage fails, the husband should examine himself. Granted, there are some men who, through no fault of their own, experience a difficult or failed marriage, but for the large majority, there is a critical need for change in attitude and actions. Often, it is the wife who encourages Bible study, church attendance, or prayer time, while men willingly forsake their God-intended role for spiritual leadership.

Speaking from personal experience and observation, many men sabotage success and their role as a leader through three destructive forces: *arrogance, addiction* and *anger.* We can either experience the momentary pain of discipline and change these destructive attitudes, or continue and experience the lasting pain of regret.

ARROGANCE

Arrogance, simply stated, reflects a silent statement that there is no need for God. It can also lead a wife to feel that she is a liability rather than an asset. Arrogance relies on self-dependence rather than dependence on God and is proud of it—get rid of it! It also signals self-centeredness. Self-centeredness leaves little room for other's needs; it stifles spiritual growth and a teachable spirit.

Without humility and a teachable spirit, relationships cannot fully develop. When our needs are more important than the needs of others, especially those of a spouse, it can severely damage a relationship. Although difficult at times, it's much easier to walk in humility than it is to stumble through life selfishly. I encourage you as a single, and when married, to build your life on godly rather than worldly wisdom. If your eyes are fixed on what the world has to offer rather than on what God has to give, an entire lifetime can be wasted.

On the lighter side, it may seem simple and understated, however a *happy wife can mean a happy life*—a happy wife is the result of a husband who is committed to the health of the relationship.

Happy wife—happy life!

ADDICTION

Addiction means to give oneself up to a habit and then become dependent upon that habit. There are many forms of addiction, from drugs and alcohol, to pornography and work or work related success. As a result, the spiritual and emotional health of the family is neglected. Workaholics, for example, can appear as hard working and industrious, but the addiction eventually robs from other relationships such as with God and family. Many men in America will accept difficult employees, face challenging situations on the job, work exhausting hours, commit fully to the cause of the company and do whatever it takes to get the job done, yet, unfortunately, severely neglect a marriage—*sometimes it appears as if they'd rather lose a wife than a career.* If this is you, as it was me, there is no greater investment than investing in your spiritual growth and the spiritual growth of your family.

Those who are addicted must seriously address the addiction before engaging in a long-term relationship—addiction consumes, and little remains for a healthy relationship. If you are a woman currently involved in a relationship with a man who shows signs of addiction, I encourage you to reconsider the relationship, quickly. Females, by nature, can be forgiving and nurturing, they tend to look beyond the faults and focus on the good. Although this disposition is certainly desirable, if it prevents a man from overcoming his addiction, it may cause more harm than good. The best recourse is to step away and allow the man to get help; if not, you become an enabler. Unfortunately, he may never fully understand or recognize the severity of his problem if others, especially you, accept his behavior.

By all means, if you are not sure if the person you are dating is prone to addiction, it is especially important to give the relationship time, and prayerfully ask for direction. (Addiction to television, video games and other seemingly innocent activities can also create problems.)

ANGER

Scripture addresses anger and our attitude toward it. Ephesians 4:31 declares, "Let all bitterness, wrath, anger, clamor, and evil speaking be put away from you . . ." Paul understood that in order for a Christian to be effective, anger would have to find its place.

Proverbs 14:17 states that "A quick-tempered man acts foolishly . . ." You may have heard the saying: *don't react instead respond*. A reaction can be emotionally charged, whereas a response can be a cognitive step of deliberate consideration. Simply stated, think before you act. A reaction often calls for an apology, while a response generally thinks things through and no apologies are needed.

Ephesians 4:26–27 says, "Be angry, and do not sin: do not let the sun go down on your wrath, nor give place to the devil." Anger over issues such as abortion, pornography and adultery is justifiable and can evoke a response with positive action. If anger causes damage to another, or personally damages character, it is not accomplishing God's purpose. If anger sparks prayer and a Christ-like stance, it's productive. James 1:20 concludes, "For the wrath of man does not produce the righteousness of God." We'll rarely settle an argument, or win a dispute with anger. We are encouraged to weigh our actions carefully and respond accordingly. Granted this is easier said than done, but it can be done with a continued reliance on God.

If not dealt with when single, many men bring anger into the marriage. As a result, wives become targets and relationships suffer. If you're a female currently dating a man who becomes easily angered, I strongly suggest that he learn to control his anger before you consider a serious commitment; this can take time. For many years, I had a difficult time controlling my temper and, at times, it's still a challenge; I have learned that anger cannot be harnessed on its own. Only the transforming Word of God and a personal relationship with Christ along with the conviction of the Holy Spirit brings life-long healing. It sounds redundant, but it's true . . . *a daily relationship with Christ through prayer and Scripture reading can eventually calm an angry spirit.* Romans 8:6 NLT states, "If your sinful nature controls your mind, there is death. But if the Holy Spirit controls your mind, there is life and peace." You'll begin to control your emotions instead of allowing your emotions to control you, and nothing feels as good as being in control.

Nothing feels as good as being in control.

In closing this chapter, one thought comes to mind: although discipline sounds difficult, it simply means to *stick to doing what is right.* With that in mind, is there really any choice?

QUESTIONS TO CONSIDER:

Is there anything in your life that is pulling you down? If so, what changes can be made?

The problem isn't that we raise our standard and miss it, it's that we lower it and hit it. Are your standards high enough?

Do you agree that discipline is simply the power to put positive choice into action?

Are you sabotaging your success through anger, addiction or arrogance? What situations should be avoided? What changes need to be made?

Memorize Psalm 1:1–3, "Blessed is the man who does not walk in the counsel of the wicked or stand in the way of sinners or sit in the seat of mockers. But his delight is in the law of the Lord, and on his law he meditates day and night. He is like a tree planted by streams of water, which yields its fruit in season and whose leaf does not wither. Whatever he does prospers" (NIV).

If you don't know where you're going, you'll probably get there.

CHAPTER FOUR

Principle

Preparation

We play like we practice

As an avid and capable athlete, my dad found great pleasure in coaching my younger brother, sister, and me in a variety of sports. Not far from our home was an open field that my grandfather helped to develop as our community's first *Little League* field. Dad's *Little League* teams and *All Stars* frequently finished league champions, or close. Practicing long, hard and often, sometimes drew complaints from weary players; his response was always . . . *we play like we practice—if we want to be champs, we practice like champs.*

Success depends not only on attitude but on preparation as well. Sports teams practice year round, corporations prepare by budgeting years in advance and many banks won't lend money without first seeing a business plan. Preparation simply means to train, to plan or to brace oneself for the future with success in mind. With that said, let's briefly shift our focus to an important aspect of preparation—*finding your purpose in life.*

FINDING YOUR PURPOSE IN LIFE— *PASSION INSPIRED BY PURPOSE*

George Barna and Mark Hatch point out in their book, *Boiling Point: It Only Takes One Degree,* that as society progresses, many will tend to lower their standards. Instead of rising beyond challenges, they will do whatever it takes to get by; with that, meaning and purpose will decrease. Without meaning and purpose, depression can easily derail our emotional and spiritual health; an important aspect of emotional health is finding purpose in life.

Searching for purpose may affect every area of life. It can determine where we'll live, whom we'll marry, where we'll work and how we'll spend our time. Unfortunately, many search for purpose and meaning in material possessions and other things that do not hold eternal value. If you believe that materially successful people are happy, think again. Most of us understand that money can buy the best mattress, but it can't guarantee sleep. Why do millionaires, movie stars and top entertainers often turn to spirituality, drugs and alcohol for the answers if success satisfies? Many discover that money, fame and recognition are not the answers. CEO's, presidents and vice presidents frequently admit that they are happy when they reach production goals, but very unhappy when under budget, *largely because they measure happiness by what's happening to them.* When things go well, they're happy, when things go poorly, they're unhappy. I'm not suggesting that we shouldn't be productive, but if happiness is measured by our circumstances, it's going to be a very rough road. One of the happiest times in my life, for example, was when I went from running multiple fitness locations to making much less money digging ditches, writing and managing nothing but my daily life. During this transition, I quickly learned that *the more I owned, the more owned me.* Goals, dreams and aspirations are God's desire for our lives, but when these things are based on self-gratification, we encounter problems emotionally, physically and spiritually.

Proverbs 13:12 states, "Hope deferred makes the heart sick, but when the desire comes, it is a tree of life." In other words, when our godly desires are fulfilled, it brings joy to our lives. The goal then is to align our desires with God's. God wants us to experience a fulfilled and abundant life, but we must look to the right source. Abundant life can include material wealth, but it does not depend upon it.

God plants desire in our heart. Without desire, one is not inclined to pursue vocations like medicine, law, professional ministry, education, construction, sales and so on. God wants us to pursue our interests. Again, He is the one who created that desire in order to serve others, but our definition of prosperity often centers on financial prosperity. III John 2 states, "Beloved, I pray that you may prosper in all things and be in health, just as your soul prospers." The statement, *as your soul prospers,* reminds us that spiritual prosperity is first and foremost; it is fundamental to our overall health and sense of well-being. In short, we can't experience true success and fulfillment without first considering the health of our soul.

Prosperity, by most definitions, means *a state of abundance.* A husband may want a large home, expensive cars and a huge bank account, but that's not what his wife needs. She needs to first feel a sense of emotional security, attention, understanding, compassion and a relationship with her husband.

Ask most men how they're doing, and they'll immediately tell you about their business, their career or their hobbies. On occasions, I've made this mistake. My pastor, Sean Appleton, brought this to my attention when he restated the question, "No, I mean how is your wife, your family and your relationship with the Lord?"

Our career, although very important, should be third in priority, following a relationship with God and our family. It's often said . . . if you want a true assessment of your priorities, simply check your calendar and checkbook. Do they need readjusting?

> *If you want a true assessment of your priorities, simply check your calendar and checkbook.*

Our passion in life should be closely interwoven with our purpose in life. Those who have a passion for teaching children, for example, often find joy as a schoolteacher. Problems arise when we seek money, status or recognition instead of the passion God has placed within us. Literally millions of single Americans (and those married) are unhappy simply because they chose a lucrative career rather than a career that they were gifted for and enjoy. Let me offer a suggestion: most colleges offer career testing and counseling, and there may be options you've never considered. You may want to take the opportunity to explore your talents and interests with a professional assessment and guidance counselor, or God may want you right where you are.

Lacking passion can be as disheartening as lacking income. The Great Depression of the early 1900's brought devastation through financial ruin. Why then does today's society experience so much unhappiness when we are at the pinnacle of financial success? It's simple . . . passion for life is directly related to purpose in life. *Many are living, but there is no life in their years.* Without God truly directing our lives, life-long fulfillment and purpose is hard to achieve. You might say, "I go to church but still lack passion." Although it helps, going to church doesn't guarantee spiritual fulfillment any more than going to the gym guarantees health. Spiritual fulfillment requires lifestyle changes and focused attention as does maintaining health.

Going to church doesn't guarantee spiritual fulfillment any more than going to the gym guarantees health.

Most of us feel depressed from time to time, simply as a result of our human condition. Physical conditions, adverse circumstances, chemical imbalances, spiritual attacks or combinations can create feelings of despair, dependency and hopelessness. How do you avoid the emotional roller coaster? First, check the obvious.

➢ Who are you associating with?

➢ What thoughts fill your mind?

➢ Are you walking in obedience to God's Word?

➢ Are you spending time in prayer and reading the Bible?

If you are doing all you know to do, and nothing seems to help, you may need professional advice. Mild depression and sadness are common to all of us, but when it lingers, it often requires more focused attention. Exercise, fun, friendship, forgiveness, kindness—all are natural chemical enhancers and can gradually help with recovery, but again, there are clear cases of clinical depression that require professional assistance.

Finding purpose in life is not a destination, it's a journey through day to day opportunities. It can be filled with unforeseen and uncharted territory, but it's a rewarding journey if you're looking to the Creator to provide the compass.

Without a vision, a journey can become mindless wandering—if you don't know where you're going you'll probably get there. Vision brings hope and direction. The Bible affirms, "Where there is no vision, the people perish . . ." (Proverbs 29:18 KJV). Ask God for purpose and vision.

> *If you don't know where you're going you'll probably get there.*

Pride will sidetrack you with thoughts such as, "I know what's best and I'll do what I want." Satan lost his position in heaven because of pride, and Eve sampled the fruit not only because it looked good, but because she was enticed by the idea of being like God. The first step in the preparation process is to ask God for direction and/or to re-align your will with His.

After You Make a Commitment to Find Purpose . . .

1. Focus on making a difference not a dollar.

Whether single, or married, those who are the most fulfilled are those who focus on making a difference in the lives of others. Focusing primarily on personal needs is a never-ending pull that satisfies only momentarily. I want to stress this point especially to men because this is where we continually fall. Proverbs 1:19 offers . . . "Such is the fate of all who are greedy for gain. It ends up robbing them of life" (NLT). To be robbed of life means to be robbed of joy, peace and contentment. Ironically, *self-centeredness takes from oneself rather than gives; it robs from life.* When we primarily seek personal gain, it affects every area of life, especially marriage.

In retrospect of my early years in the fitness industry, I found that when I focused on earning a large paycheck, I wasn't fulfilled; however, when I focused on helping others, I was fulfilled. You've heard it said, and I quickly learned, *that people don't care how much you know until they know how much you care*—kindness can be more impressive than a paycheck, and it's more fulfilling. Focus on making a positive difference in the lives of others; you'll never regret that decision.

2. Focus on character instead of charisma.

Charisma describes a magnetic and alluring personality. I'm not referring to a general spiritual charismatic experience or positive character traits; I'm referring to those who are charming for the purpose of personal gain. Charisma might be inclined to be politically correct, to fit in, or to say what others want to hear, whereas good character is steadfast, unchanging and supports what is right rather than what is popular. Worldly charisma is a charm that deceives by outer appearance for the sake of personal gain. Godly character has the quality of a gracious heart that seeks to find and bring out the best in others, for the sake of others.

3. Don't compete . . . complement.

This principle may seem extreme, especially in America where competition is commonplace. However, in regard to finding fulfillment, competition can be counter-productive. To compete actually means to fight, struggle, contend or battle with. This doesn't sound appealing does it? While the concept of "healthy competition" relates well to sports events, in marriage it can be close to an oxymoron unless it involves trying to outdo the other in developing positive partnering skills.

Complement means to balance, harmonize or go to together. For example, if two sales associates are working in the same office selling the same product, it's much healthier and more beneficial to work together in harmony than it is to struggle and contend for sales all day. This isn't easy, I know. At one point I supervised over a hundred sales personnel and competition was a large factor. Those who stopped fighting and worked as a team while pursuing their goals were, by far, the happiest as well as the most productive employees. There was no need to compete or scratch their way to the top. Many of these employees were successful because they knowingly or unknowingly received the Proverbs 18:16 blessing, "A man's gift make's room for him . . ."

MAKING ROOM OR TAKING UP SPACE?

God gives each of us gifts to give away. For example, I have a desire to help others in the area of health and fitness, largely because I experienced the effects of poor nutrition. I also have a desire to help others with relationships because I experienced the pain of divorce.

God has called us all to be part of a large, collective body that minister to one another. Some may have gifts of teaching, administration, preaching or leading. They may have been called to be a businessman, a technician, a pastor, an actress, etc. Problems arise when we try to be what we are not. For instance, if God has called you to work with children and you're

Problems arise when we try to be what we are not.

spending your time as a business professional, fulfillment may be hard to come by. On the other hand, some are doing what they love but still lack fulfillment, largely because of their definition of success. For example, a singer may cut demo tapes and promote their music, but their career doesn't take off. They see other artists succeed and wonder why they're not. Maybe the question shouldn't be, *why am I not succeeding,* but rather, *am I pursuing my God-given purpose,* and *how am I measuring success?* Maybe they should redefine success. Is there a difference between an artist who sells millions of CD's worldwide and whose music videos reach the top ten, compared to the person who sings at church, touches dozens of lives and attends to the daily needs of his or her family? Society may believe that there is a huge

> *God looks at the heart rather than outward appearance.*

difference; one is a "success" the other is not, but God looks at the heart rather than outward appearance (1 Samuel 16:7 paraphrased). It may be that both are successful in His eyes. Surely He blesses people with prosperity and recognition, but in many cases, the one who appears least is actually greater. Simply ask yourself, *"Am I trying to do my best,* or *be the best?"* Doing your best and being the best can spring from different motives. When we try to "be the best" we may have the tendency to compete and compromise our character, thus lowering our standards in the pursuit of being number one, or rising to the top. Strive for excellence and make every effort to accomplish your goals, but check your method and motives.

When your gift makes room for you, it may not reflect society's definition of success, but it will produce joy, peace and fulfillment.

Using your gifts to help others will help you find contentment, no matter what the circumstance. Is it always easy? Not at all! But when we reflect on how blessed we are as a nation and how gracious God has been, we can be immediately encouraged and motivated to continue.

In closing, from time to time, you may feel helpless and depressed even when you're doing all that you know to do. You may even lose confidence in your ability, and feel like giving up and returning to your familiar comfort zone. DON'T! This thinking is wrong! Press through. You are exercising the very important muscle of perseverance. There is a saying that ships are safest in the harbor, but they are not made for the harbor. Likewise, you were designed to weather storms successfully.

> *You were not created to fail—you were created to succeed.*

When life becomes difficult and challenging, set your sites on the goal not on the challenge. You were not created to fail, you were created to succeed—and make sure you remember the true meaning of "success". There is a blessing just beyond the circumstance. Simply trust that God is leading despite appearances and keep moving forward.

It can be easier to prepare for physical exertion than to prepare for the mental exertion of relationships: use the calmer times of your life to prepare for the challenges ahead, not only physically, but also mentally; read, rest and practice patience in the little things. Much like an athlete who prepares all year for the one-day event, he or she doesn't win the event in one day; it is a gradual practice of preparation, discipline and perseverance. Little disciplines, practiced day-by-day, produce winning results—we play like we practice.

YOUR MOST IMPORTANT JOB—*MEN AND WOMEN*

On a final note, in preparing for the future, it's wise to consider your role as a parent, whether single or dating. Do you and your potential spouse agree on this role? If not, now is the time to discuss it.

If you are a parent, or plan to be one, your greatest investment will be in your children. Your goal may be to own a business, climb the corporate ladder or pursue a profession; whatever your career choice, there is no greater opportunity than to promote the spiritual success of another, especially if that person is your child.

A few decades ago, being a devoted mother was viewed as the most important job one could have. Society understood the famous quote

PRINCIPLE FOUR:

PREPARATION

"The hand that rocks the cradle is the hand that rules the world" (W. R. Wallace), and thus, promoted parenthood. Not so today. Many women feel worthless without a career. It is a misconception that a stay-at-home parent has a minimal job. My mother, for example, postponed her profession until we were raised, and for that we are deeply grateful. While at home raising three children, she was active in the community and helped my father with our family business, but she felt her greatest priority was in assuring the well being of her family. My father made time in the evenings and weekends helping with sports and other activities.

Qualities such as honesty, integrity, commitment, discipline and a strong work ethic are not easily taught or transmitted through mere words; they are instilled through lives that model these traits. The involvement of both parents in the lives of their children helps to impart values through modeled behavior.

While growing up, I took a temporary detour. However, my parents' examples left an indelible impression. I'll be forever thankful for the time we shared, the lessons I learned and the person I became as a result of the time we spent together. *Never underestimate the power of parenting!*

Make no mistake about it, we live in a society that emphasizes wealth and what we posses, and we often fail to remember that these things have no eternal value. I don't remember my father's income or many of the physical things my parents gave to me. I do, however, remember the values they taught—those things that money cannot buy. They taught me that success is not measured by what we have, but rather by what we give. It's been well stated that "the best things in life aren't things".

Success is not measured by what we have, but rather by what we give.

It's possible to succeed in business but fail at home. Look around, it's happening everywhere, from the pulpit to the boardroom. Unfortunately, the price of success is often paid at the expense of the family. A friend, Pastor Jim Girdlestone, relayed a tragic story. He told of a recent trip to the hospital to visit a man who was dying. The man could no longer speak, he could, however, write. His desire was to be taken off life-support, but what followed was more devastating. The man cried as he wrote. At the top of his list, he regretted that he had not spent more time with his family. He was in anguish over the fact that he had not been a better father, but instead, had built his life around other things. When all is said and done, it is devastating to find that life was invested in those things that hold no lasting value.

Some research indicates that the average American father actually "listens" to his children only minutes a day. A decision on our part to maintain proper priorities can solve that problem. Don't let the pursuit of a career take precedence over your family. Be deliberate in planning time for your family—*if you don't schedule time, it will schedule for you.*

Family Friend

In planning ahead for parenthood, give thought to who and what will influence your children. The following story may hold little resemblance to the original; nevertheless, it successfully describes an American dilemma.

When Matt was just four years old, his parents introduced him to a new friend. He was excited because he had someone to play with, and they were happy because their friend could baby-sit when they were busy.

As the years went by, Matt and his friend spent countless hours together playing video games and watching sports. In time, things changed. His friend began to use profanity and show disrespect to his family. Although his mother and father disapproved, what could they do? His friend was like a family member now. He taught Matt how to dress, how to act and even how to treat others; and although his parents wouldn't admit it, he taught them a thing or two as well. He promoted the importance of career and money; he encouraged Matt's mom to pursue her dreams outside the home, and his father to continue his pursuit of financial success. Sadly enough, they listened to his advice; as a result, Matt rarely saw his parents.

Once Matt reached his teen years, his friend's influence was obvious. Matt spent more time with him than with his family. Since Matt's dad was always gone, his friend taught him how to be a father and a husband, and since his mom was busy most of the time, he offered to teach Matt about women, and how to treat them.

When Matt was fourteen, his friend introduced him to sex. He explained that it wasn't a bad thing; everybody was doing it, even with same sex partners. At this point, Matt's parents became upset and warned Matt not to see his friend again, but he couldn't end the relationship—he'd been his close companion for the past decade. Surprisingly, Matt's parents allowed his friend to continue to live in their home. After all, they enjoyed his company and didn't really want to see him leave—he was a great entertainer.

During the years that followed, Matt's friend introduced him to alcohol, drugs and pornography, and again assured him that everyone was doing it. Matt could see his friend's point; he showed him literally thousands of people who agreed with this lifestyle.

When Matt grew older, he looked back over the years and saw that the friendship should never have continued. He believed that his friend's influence encouraged his father's affair, his mom's problem with alcohol and it may have ultimately contributed to their divorce. His friend's impact on his life was just as devastating.

Today, with full knowledge of the damage done, Matt still allows his friend to live with him, and, amazingly, he still listens to his advice. Matt's friend has a name, it's *television.*

Although there are negative influences other than television, *Family Friend* proves a powerful point, "For as he thinks in his heart, so is he . . ." (Proverbs 23:7). Seriously consider how you spend your time, and how your children will spend their time. Some believe that TV reflects society more than it influences it, and that we should strengthen the listener rather than silence the messenger, however, the following suggests otherwise . . .

➤ On average, American families watch over seven hours of TV a day. Yes, seven hours. The book, *TV—The Great Escape,* confirms that most television programs are reshaping the moral structure of our society by lowering the standards in which we view others and ourselves.

➤ TV programs often undermine respect and the integrity of individuals.

➤ Television takes quality time from relationships, mainly marriages, and ongoing investments with children. In brief, television, on average, fills the mind with an unproductive, unrealistic outlook on life. (For those who are skeptical that the media influences our actions, consider why companies pay millions of dollars for commercials during the Super Bowl.)

Am I suggesting that you rid your homes of television? That's for you to decide. If you do decide to enjoy it on occasion, I suggest watching it sparingly, and view programs that offer healthy entertainment and important news updates. Unfortunately, that list is small, very small.

TIMELESS TIPS

Again, preparation simply means to train, to plan or to brace oneself for the future with success in mind. We are reminded throughout Scripture to be prepared; Proverbs offers timeless advice. (References are taken from the New Living Translation Bible.)

Be prepared by . . .

Acquiring Wisdom

Proverbs 1:4 . . . **"These Proverbs will make the simpleminded clever. They will give knowledge and purpose to young people."** God promises that reading and applying Proverbs to our lives will give wisdom and purpose, however reading alone doesn't guarantee success, application does.

Walking In Integrity

Proverbs 2:7 . . . **"He grants a treasure of good sense to the godly. He is their shield, protecting those who walk with integrity."**

Seeking And Trusting Him

Proverbs 3:5–6 . . . **"Trust in the Lord with all your heart; do not depend on your own understanding. Seek His will in all you do, and he will direct your paths."**

Setting Your Sites

Proverbs 4:25–27 . . . **"Look straight ahead, and fix your eyes on what lies before you. Mark out a straight path for your feet; then stick to the path and stay safe. Don't get sidetracked; keep your feet from following evil."**

Avoiding These Things

Proverbs 6:17–19 lists seven things that the Lord hates . . .

1. Haughty eyes (Pride or arrogance.)

2. A lying tongue

3. Hands that kill the innocent

4. A heart that plots evil

5. Feet that race to do wrong

6. A false witness who pours out lies

7. A person who sows discord among brothers

Exercising Power Through Patience

Proverbs 16:32 . . . **"It is better to be patient than powerful; it is better to have self-control than to conquer a city."** Patient people deliberately take their time to examine the possibilities, weigh the consequences, seek guidance if necessary and do what they believe to be right. Self-control allows us to control our desires and emotions rather than allowing them to control us.

Trusting His Lead

Proverbs 20:24 . . . **"How can we understand the road we travel? It is the Lord who directs our steps."** We will never fully understand the complexities of life; simply trust God and faithfully follow His lead.

Taking No Shortcuts To Success

Proverbs 21:5 . . . **"Good planning and hard work lead to prosperity, but hasty shortcuts lead to poverty."**

Choosing Reputation Over Riches

Proverbs 22:1 . . . **"Choose a good reputation over great riches, for being held in high esteem is better than having silver or gold."** Don't jeopardize reputation for money. If a challenging decision needs to be made, let integrity guide you, not profit.

I encourage you to use the book of Proverbs as a daily study. One helpful way to study Proverbs is to read the chapter that corresponds with the day of the month. For example, read Proverbs 1 on the first day of the month, and so on.

PRE-PLANNED MEANS PREPARED

In your journal, take the time now to plan for success. How are you preparing for dating, marriage, parenthood, a career change or other changes? Will you purchase reputable resource books and a good study Bible, pay down bills, etc.? For example, you may want to visit www.familylife.com or www.family.org (i.e., FOCUS ON THE FAMILY) and review their list of resources. (Visit www.whydietsdontwork.com for help with weight-loss and fitness.)

JOURNAL EXAMPLE:

1. Spiritual growth:	6 a.m.—prayer/Bible study/journal
2. Family:	7 a.m.—time with family
3. Health & fitness:	8 a.m.—exercise

And so on . . .

Begin with a plan. You will have to make adjustments for unexpected events, but get back on track as soon as possible. In 30 days, evaluate again. If not on track, decide how you can prepare for the next 30 days. List your short-term and long-term goals and refer to them often. This will help you stay focused.

QUESTIONS TO CONSIDER:

Do you agree that many people search for purpose and meaning in material possessions and other things that have no eternal value? Why is this counterproductive?

Do you often measure happiness by your circumstances? How can this hinder peace and joy?

Do you often try to do your best, or be the best?

Assess your priorities by reviewing your calendar and checkbook. Do they need readjusting?

Problems arise when we try to be what we are not. What abilities and gifts has God given you? Are you making the best use of them?

When life becomes difficult and challenging, do you set your sites on the goal or the challenge?

If you are a parent or plan to be one, your greatest investment will be in your children. How can you begin to, or continue, investing in their development?

Memorize Proverbs 1:19, "Such is the fate of all who are greedy for gain. It ends up robbing them of life" (NLT).

Poor choices take us farther than we want to go, cost us more than we want to pay and keep us longer than we want to stay!

CHAPTER FIVE

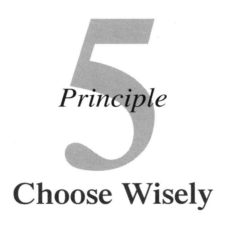

Principle

Choose Wisely

Dating & courting
Quality of choice today affects the quality of life tomorrow

Michelle was raised in what many would consider to be a good Christian home. She began dating at sixteen and held high standards for her relationships. She met and dated Mark while they were in college. He told her that he was a Christian and that he valued and respected her standards; he also mentioned that he had been with a few girls but that he felt differently about her. The fact that he had been involved sexually bothered her initially, but he reassured her that it wouldn't happen in their relationship.

They continued to date and Michelle stopped attending church. She also lost interest in reading her Bible, and prayer was no longer a priority. Mark eventually convinced Michelle to spend the night and she gave in to his advances. She was devastated. Her only comfort was in believing that Mark felt as she did, especially now, and would marry her. She was wrong. Within a month, Mark was gone and Michelle was emotionally shattered—she had given away the gift that she had resolved would be given to only one person.

What Can Be Learned from Michelle's Experience?

➢ Michelle should have regarded Mark's actions rather than His Words. Mark's personal agenda manipulated Michelle—he told her what she wanted to hear. *Actions still speak louder than words.*

➢ Michelle's relationship distracted her from God. Rather than continuing to grow spiritually, she invested more time in Mark and other activities. She should have followed wholeheartedly after Christ and seen if he kept up.

➢ When Mark asked Michelle to spend the night, he revealed his motives, no guess work was involved. The enemy didn't push Michelle off the ledge; he took her down one step at a time, one compromise at a time, one mistake at a time. Simply stated, *take control while you are still in control.*

> *Take control while you're still in control.*

➢ Michelle thought that she would someday marry Mark. This false assumption allowed Mark to edge his way into her heart. Michelle should have guarded her heart and realized that even though she may someday marry him, sex before marriage was not an option.

➢ When Michelle separated herself from God's presence, and His protection, she had two choices: to *fall backward* or to *fall forward.* Had she chosen to fall forward into God's forgiveness, in time God's grace would have healed and restored her. Although there are negative consequences for poor choices, there are also positive consequences for wise choices. When confronted by sin, God wants us to fall forward and run to Him, not away.

> *God wants us to fall forward and run to Him, not away!*

➢ Fortunately, despite her circumstances, Michelle was free to ask for forgiveness and position herself, once again, in the center of God's will.

This illustration focused on Michelle's choices; however Mark's list of irresponsible actions was just as long; can you spot them?

WHEN YOU FALL—FALL FORWARD

If you're making wrong choices, STOP! Begin to make right choices and establish solid footing once again. There may be consequences, but through forgiveness there is restoration.

If we could clearly see where sin was leading, most of us would probably reconsider our options. The enemy blinds us to the consequences of sin and entices us with its pleasures. If one could see that one, "harmless" little sexual sin would lead to adultery, divorce, separation from children, depression and despair, he or she would probably change the behavior in a heartbeat. *We're often too smart to take large, deliberate plunges, but we can be enticed to take one step at a time, one compromise at a time, one sin at a time—until it's too late!*

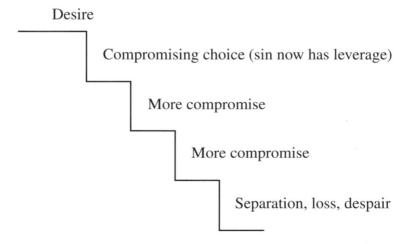

When the Bible describes sin as a path that leads to death, it's describing separation from God; death simply means *separation.* Sexual sin often results in the death of a family, a marriage and the integrity of an individual. The entire family loses. That's what sin does; it draws the life out of you and those closest to you. According to John 10:10, the enemy comes to steal, to kill and to

> *When you fall—*
> *fall forward.*

destroy our relationship with God, and thus, with others (paraphrased). Unwise choices and/or relationships promote destruction. Conversely, right choices and positive relationships promote health and growth. Consider your choices. And again, *when you fall, fall forward!*

We Can't "Un-Know" What We Have Known

References to sexual experiences in the Bible are sometimes defined as "he knew his wife." To *know*, in this context, is to know intimately through sexual experience. Regrettably, for those who experience sex before marriage, it is impossible to un-know what is known. Sexual experiences cannot be un-done. Each time we engage in premarital sex, we add additional emotional weight to our lives, and it's difficult to run a marital marathon while carrying the extra weight of regret from past relationships.

Weakness means the absence of strength, whereas meekness means strength under control. Those who refrain from sex before marriage exhibit far more strength than those who don't. In essence, it takes more strength to say no than to say yes. Isn't that the case in so many areas of life?

As men, we are called to be the leaders in the relationship. Don't place the burden of leadership on the one you are dating—demonstrate self-control in the area of abstinence. When we display this type of discipline, we compliment her as someone of great value and respect. A word of caution to women, if the man you are dating is not concerned with purity (despite your past), reconsider the relationship—*if he's not concerned with doing what's right now, he may not be concerned about protecting you in other areas once married.* Although a man may find you attractive, his motivation to protect your purity, and his, should outweigh his desire for sex. If it doesn't . . . you fill in the blank.

If you've stumbled in this area, don't keep stumbling from this point forward—God will reward your obedience. There is hope and healing for those who desire it. Unmistakably, the quality of your choice today will affect the quality of your life tomorrow. If you desire a good marriage or a fulfilled single life in the future, it begins with the right choice today. For those who have chosen to postpone sexual intimacy, it will be worth the wait. Ask yourself, "Do I want to experience the temporary pain of discipline or the lasting pain of regret?"

The quality of your choice today will affect the quality of your life tomorrow.

Let me restate my point. If you're currently involved in this type of relationship, understand that it's not where God wants you to be. *He cannot bless a decision to continue in a sexual relationship, which the Bible refers to as fornication, but He can bless a decision to repent and abstain until marriage.* Pre-marital sex robs the couple of a level of intimacy and closeness reserved for life-long commitment. Sex was designed by God to enhance an intimate, lasting, committed marriage.

TOO CLOSE TO THE EDGE

Without a doubt, the largest factor contributing to the destruction of many relationships (including marriage) is the lack of sexual purity. Why then do so many continue to fall in this area? I vividly remember a message by Bishop T.D. Jakes delivered to a group of prisoners at San Quinton Prison (Tape Series: *Prison Breaking Truths*). In regard to repeating destructive behavior, many asked why they chronically found themselves back in prison. Bishop Jakes told the story of a young boy who kept falling out of his bed week after week. When the boy asked his mother why he kept falling, she wisely answered, "It's because you don't get far enough in!" In the same way, *many of us fall back into sin because we're too close to the edge and we don't move far enough in to God's framework of safety and protection.*

Overcoming sin, especially sexual sin, can be a difficult battle for Christians. On one hand, the Apostle Paul declares, "Our old sinful selves were crucified with Christ so that sin might lose its power in our lives . . ." (Romans 6:6 NLT). Yet, in the next chapter he states, "For the good that I will to do, I do not do; but the evil I will not to do, that I practice" (Romans 7:19 NKJ). His lament continues in verse twenty-four, "Oh, what a miserable person I am! Who will free me from this life that is dominated by sin?" (NLT). It leaves one to wonder that *if I'm dead to sin why is it still alive in me?* How can Paul declare that he is dead to sin in one verse, yet also ask *who will free me from the domination of sin in my life?* In addition, Romans 6:16 (NLT) states, ". . . that whatever you choose to obey becomes your master? You can choose sin, which leads to death, or you can choose to obey God and receive His approval."

Paul was not saying that he has no power over sin; he was saying that, on his own, he is defenseless. The next verse reads, ". . . Once you were slaves of sin . . ." (6:17 NLT). A slave is one who is owned by another, or dominated by some influence. When Paul says that his life is dominated by sin; he's declaring that life here on earth is strongly influenced by the enemy. Sin is present in this world, but its power over us was crucified when we accepted Christ's sacrifice. *Do we position ourselves to be drawn away by the strong pull of sin, or do we align ourselves to be firmly footed on solid ground?* Isaiah 7:9 instructs, ". . . If you do not stand firm in your faith, you will not stand at all" (NIV).

> *If you do not stand firm in your faith, you will not stand at all.*
> —Isaiah 7:9 (NIV)

The only way to stand against the enemy is to stand strong in your faith. A half-hearted approach stands on unstable ground. Where are you standing?

Paul also states, "Do not let sin control the way you live; do not give in to its lustful desires" (Romans 6:12 NLT). As noted earlier, whatever we feed grows, and what grows will largely control our lives. This is a concept that cognitive-behavioral therapists clearly understand—*behavioral changes begin with a change in thoughts;* therefore, Philippians 4:8 encourages us to fix our thoughts on what is true and honorable and right, and to think about things that are pure, lovely, admirable, excellent and worthy of praise (paraphrased).

Let me offer a word of encouragement; if this all seems overwhelming and you are having difficulty breaking old patterns, begin with what you *can* do. That one choice will soon fuel the desire for other positive choices. As an example, if you can't *subtract* a negative such as a bad attitude, for now, *add* Scripture study and prayer in that area. If you can't give up chocolate, add an afternoon vegetable plate with low-fat dip. The encouragement of taking steps in a positive direction can fuel the flame to take more positive steps—positive energy creates more positive energy. A change in attitude often means a change in action.

> *A change in attitude often means a change in action.*

James 1:14–15 offers, "But each one is tempted when he is drawn away by his own desires and enticed. Then, when desire has conceived, it gives birth to sin; and sin, when it is full-grown, brings forth death." To be *drawn away* is to be enticed to do something. The problem isn't necessarily knowing what to do; it's doing what we know. For instance,

> *The problem isn't necessarily knowing what to do; it's doing what we know.*

many know that sex outside of marriage is wrong, but the desire for sex is often stronger than the desire to obey spiritual principles. The pull of sex is everywhere and like a fishing lure, we don't often notice the hook until we take the bait. Scan the channels on TV, view the covers of many magazines, listen to the radio, glance at the billboards that crowd our freeways and at the movie covers that fill our video stores—sex surrounds us. Consequently, *the more we feed this desire, the more we'll have to fight this desire.* In most cases, men are more vulnerable in the area of what they see and think, and women in what they hear and feel. With that in mind, here are a few suggestions . . .

1. Avoid **looking** intentionally at things that stimulate lust. There are times when we cannot avoid what we see: a person walking by, a commercial on TV or an unannounced Internet page that suddenly emerges on the screen. Temptation is not sin, but what we do with it can be. Matthew 6:22–23 states that "The lamp of the body is the eye. If therefore your eye is good, your whole body will be full of light. But if your eye is bad, your whole body will be full of darkness . . ." What we choose to look at determines where our thoughts will go; determine beforehand to avoid looking at things that can stimulate lust.

2. Avoid **places** that stimulate lust. I remember reading an article about a man who began avoiding the beach in the summer after admitting his addiction to pornography to his wife. He concluded that being around people who were barely covered often triggered his compulsion. Another case involved a woman who stopped visiting the romance section at her local bookstore; she also concluded that reading romance novels was stimulating unhealthy lust. Although these examples may seem extreme, to reduce lust, we must avoid places, people or things that stimulate that desire. *It often begins with a small compromise, which leads to another, and another.* When possible, simply avoid places that trigger wrong desires.

PRINCIPLE FIVE:

CHOOSE WISELY

3. Avoid **saying** things that stimulate lust. Proverbs 18:21 reminds us that "Death and life are in the power of the tongue . . ." Are your words, at times, giving life to lust? If so, rethink what you're about to say before you say it. Ask yourself if what you are about to say will strengthen your partner's walk with the Lord and yours, or draw you away.

4. Avoid **listening** to things that stimulate lust. Much of today's music, for example, can be incredibly sexual in nature; it encourages thoughts that can draw us away from God's presence. Music is a compelling force and lyrics continually place thoughts in our minds. *As thoughts grow, actions often follow.* What you choose to listen to is vitally important. Whether it's listening to others or to the media, pay close attention to whom and what you listen to.

5. The power of **touch** creates incredible feelings. God designed this feeling to be shared within in its proper context. Many view dating or courting as a license to touch without restriction. Not only is it important to place boundaries around what we see, hear and say, we need also to be careful with touch. Many Christian leaders suggest that holding hands be the only type of touching a couple displays until they move into courting. After that, only light, non-sexual touching is recommended. I know this may sound radical, but extreme or not, sex starts with a touch. One touch leads to another, and another, until we make a wrong choice. Remember, *if you don't control your desires, your desires will control you.* One of the best ways to control desire is by controlling touch.

SHOULD I DATE OR COURT?

Is there a difference? Dating provides opportunity to spend time together and suggests it can be short or long-term; courting infers a long-term commitment with marriage in mind. Today's secular dating practices, largely encouraged by the media, focus on fulfilling one's sexual desires as a primary goal in the relationship. The goal should be to build a strong, meaningful relationship, and to do what is right instead of labeling the relationship. Rather than asking should I date or court, ask, *"What should I do while dating or courting?"* Whether dating or courting, God desires an exchange of respect, honesty, self-control and attitudes that nurture a positive relationship. The goal is to follow His design for relationships. Simply stated, *the term used isn't as important as character demonstrated during the process.* Regardless of whether you are dating or courting, consider these guidelines . . .

> *Dating or courting . . . the term used isn't as important as character demonstrated during the process.*

➤ Underscore patience instead of expedience.

➤ Incorporate daily Bible study and prayer as a discipline.

➤ Seek godly counsel before and during the relationship.

➤ Share the same spiritual beliefs; be equally yoked.

➤ Interact in a variety of settings and circumstances while minimizing time alone.

➤ Spend time together a day or two a week initially; slowly add more time.

➤ Avoid situations that can fuel sexual desire.

➤ Spend time in different situations and social settings to help determine compatibility.

Think for a moment, any good friendship with a male or female can offer just about anything a marriage can: a life-long relationship, cohabitation, shared travel and interests, shared expenses and so on. What is left to set marriage apart? It makes sense that God would create one act that distinguishes marriage from all other relationships, one that would provide the "glue" that binds and holds together. A relationship that is firmly anchored creates a stable environment in which to raise children and sustain commitment. Sexual intimacy was not designed to be a recreational sport; it was intended to create a spiritual bond that would assure that "the two shall become one," and remain as one (Genesis 2:24 paraphrased). In Dr. James Dobson's book, *Love For A Lifetime*, he discusses the research findings of Dr. Desmond Morris conveyed through the writings of Dr. Donald Joy. He states, "Bonding refers to the emotional covenant that links a man and women together for life and makes them intensely valuable to one another. It is the specialness that sets those two lovers apart from every other couple on the face of the earth."

Had Morgan and I experienced sexual intimacy with one another before marriage, we would have lost something that God had designed for us to share only as a married couple—we may have ended the relationship due to the lack of trust and respect. *It's sobering to think that my loving wife may have been a past regret.* This is not to say that couples who fail to wait can't have a blessed marriage, but God wants to spare us the added pain that comes with living in disobedience.

As a word of hope, although past sexual experiences cannot be reversed, our mind and spirit can be renewed and restored. Don't allow past mistakes to cause future pain. If God is calling you back to a place of purity and wholeness, don't become discouraged and despondent because of past failure. Recognize that *those who have been forgiven much, love much* (Luke 7:47 paraphrased). This change in attitude and action is not only pleasing to God, but it will help you attract the right qualities in others as you pursue a lifelong partner.

HOW FAR IS TOO FAR—A FUTURE SPOUSE OR A PAST REGRET

A George Barna poll stated that 36 percent of self-proclaimed, born-again Christians approve of living together before marriage, and 39 percent said that sex before marriage is morally acceptable (FOCUS ON THE FAMILY magazine, February 2002). An even larger number, despite their beliefs, have experienced sex outside of marriage. Why do so many people fall in this area? I believe that, often, *the motivation to abstain from sex does not outweigh the desire to heed God's direction,* or some believe that God is indifferent. To regain our balance, we need to continually do those things that strengthen our relationship with Him.

Please understand that I'm not trying to overwhelm you, but the consequences of sexual sin can be tragic. Consider, alone, the growing epidemic of sexually transmitted diseases, abortion and unwanted pregnancies. If we candy-coat this issue and fail to see it for what it is, we can easily be misled. Unfortunately, many forget that poor choices have long-term consequences.

> *Many forget that poor choices have long-term consequences.*

As a word of encouragement, if you feel that you've been defeated in the area of sexual abstinence, simply ask God for forgiveness, repent and fall forward—God is faithful to forgive and redirect you. The enemy desires to take what God has designed for good and distort it. It's been said *that we cannot defeat an enemy that we cannot see;* we also cannot defeat an enemy that we are not prepared for. For that reason, we're often caught off guard; therefore, it's critical to establish a commitment before a serious relationship begins, such as: "Because we have committed our relationship to God and ourselves, and because I care for you, we are not going to do. . . ." Joseph ran from Potiphar's wife and cried, ". . . How then can I do this great wickedness, and sin against God?"

His motivation to serve God was the key to his success.

(Genesis 39:9). He didn't say that he wasn't attracted to her; he said *how can I sin against my Lord*. His motivation to serve God was the key to his success.

It's critical to identify areas of vulnerability early and to avoid them at all costs. If our lives are clouded by sin, it will be difficult to hear clearly from God. Enlist an accountability couple or person whom you can communicate with on a regular basis. Prior to marriage, Morgan and I talked often with trusted friends who would ask the difficult questions such as how we were doing sexually.

If we respect and honor others the way God intended, we'll either gain a godly spouse or learn from the experience. However, if we misuse His gift, a potential spouse may instead become a past regret. The current trend of divorce and marital problems may be a reflection of the violation of this principle. *Becoming sexually involved before marriage does not only cloud the judgment of the couple before marriage, but can also feed thoughts of mistrust and doubt later.*

One theme that appears common among the experts is this: *when we become sexually stimulated either physically or mentally, we begin to sin.* Once we are convicted within our spirit, we can rest assured that our behavior borders on being sinful. At that point, we have the option to move toward or away. Take Paul's advice and "flee sexual immorality . . ." (1 Corinthians 6:18)—flee is the key!

When considering how far is too far, don't take chances. If it feels like temptation, it probably is. Treat others with dignity and respect by not causing them to stumble— they may some day be your spouse.

If it feels like temptation, it probably is.

Is There Only One Person for Me?

This question is often asked and there is no clear-cut answer. I'm reminded of the story found in Luke 19:11–27. A master gave his servants talents to invest. Two of the servants invested wisely and took care of what had been given to them. The last servant hid the talent and did nothing with it. As a result, he lost it. We, too, are equally entrusted with gifts and freedom with how we are to invest, whether financially, relationally or physically. Ultimately, it is our decision as to what we do with our gifts. Some may even have the gift of singleness; yes, it's a gift; ask those who are happily single, or unhappily married.

If you are seeking God wholeheartedly, praying for a godly spouse, walking morally upright and are a good steward of the gifts that He has given you, I believe that you will be offered His best, whether it's singleness or marriage—God will reward you as you honor Him.

> *God will reward you as you honor Him.*

For those who are divorced, the question, *"Does God have just one person for me?"* takes on new meaning and there is no "one size fits all" response. Although God forgives, loves and supports us, there are consequences for our actions—apart from forgiveness. If the divorce causes us to draw closer to God and we become better not bitter, He will reward and redeem our lives. God knows your heart and can bless the situation regardless of the circumstances surrounding the divorce. (See the chapter *Broken—yet Unbreakable*).

Finding and Being Found: Your Role in the Pursuit

The account of Abraham's servant who sought a wife for Isaac in Genesis 24:2–51 (NLT) offers wonderful insight in defining our role in the pursuit and finding God's best for our lives.

1. Once God makes His direction clear, don't compromise. Abraham's servant was told where to go. He didn't visit local nightclubs or singles' bars; he followed the instruction to go back to his homeland and find a wife. Abraham wanted a wife for his son who knew the Lord. "Swear . . . that you will not let my son marry one of these local Canaanite women. Go instead to my homeland, to my relatives, and find a wife there for my son Isaac" (24:3–4). Abraham wanted Isaac to marry someone who shared his heritage, and thus, his beliefs. Had Isaac married a Canaanite, he may easily have embraced their false gods and been led astray. In this, Abraham teaches the principle of an equal yoke. Although Abraham lived in the city with unbelievers, he did not want his son to be joined with one. For that reason, we should seek in places pleasing to the Lord.

   We should seek in places pleasing to the Lord.

2. We read in verse ten that *the servant loaded Abraham's camels with gifts and took with him the best of everything his master owned.* The servant went out prepared to be a blessing. When you enter into a relationship, whether male or female, determine to be a blessing no matter the length of the relationship. Today's culture tends to ask, "What can I get from this relationship?" rather than, "What can I give to this relationship?" Enter the relationship intending to bring. When you give, ultimately you receive.

3. Next, we read in verse fifteen, that *as he was still praying, a young woman named Rebekah arrived with a water jug on her shoulder.* Prayer preceded the blessing.

4. Verse sixteen identifies Rebekah as a virgin. A desire for sexual purity is fundamental in finding the right person or being found by the right person. I want to encourage those who are virgins to remain so, and those who are not, to make a decision to abstain until marriage. The desire to remain sexually pure until marriage must be at the top of the list. We may not understand why, but God does not give meaningless directives. Had Rebekah had previous sexual encounters, although we don't know for sure, Abraham's servant may not have been led to her; she might have missed God's blessing for her life. Remember, despite your past, God redeems.

   Despite your past, God redeems.

5. Verse twenty-one states that *the servant watched her in silence, wondering whether or not she was the one the Lord intended him to meet.* In deciding whether to date or to continue dating, take time and observe the attitudes and behaviors of the other. Are they inclined to serve, or to be served? Are they critical, argumentative or defensive? Give yourself time to observe their disposition, and remember that most will be on their best behavior, at least initially. Observe them around their family, children, when under pressure and when upset. Also observe how a son treats his mother and a daughter her father as an indicator of potential strengths and weaknesses.

6. Once the servant knew that he had found the right person, he thanked God and praised Him (Genesis 24:26–27). How many times do we forget to thank God for guiding and leading us? We should constantly thank Him and ask for His continued direction in our lives. In summary, we might say: *don't compromise, choose one who shares your beliefs, bless others, pray, seek to remain pure, be observant* and *be thankful.*

Timeless Principles

God offers timeless principles that can save us from ourselves as we pursue a relationship.

➤ He stresses patience—we want it now.

➤ He wants to prepare us—we think we're ready.

➤ He wants to train us—we want to do it our way.

➤ He wants what's best for us—we'll take second best.

➤ He wants to mold us into His image—we're more concerned with self-image.

You can see where this is going. It's all about us, and what we want. Recognize that there is a Master Builder who has a plan.

Don't rush the process and waste time trying to find someone or something. When we rush, we can waste time and bring unneeded anxiety into our lives. Whether you're sixteen and beginning to date, or sixty-six and healing from divorce, the search for Mr. or Miss "Right" may be a priority. It's difficult to wait for Mr. or Miss "Right"; most want *Mr. or Miss "Right Now".* More important than learning how to find Mr. or Miss

Many focus on finding someone special without first understanding the need to become someone special.

Right is learning how to be Mr. or Miss Right; dating is not only about attracting the opposite sex, it's about attracting the right qualities in others. Many focus on finding someone special without first understanding the need to become someone special. Again, the principle of *reaping* and *sowing* relates not only to financial success, it relates to success with others as well. If one desires to find a trustworthy, and committed person, he or she must also offer those qualities. Today's society often promotes the opposite. Character qualities such as honesty, integrity, commitment, perseverance and serving are almost non-existent. As a result, marriages are failing, families disintegrating and relationships ending, simply because society endorses meeting self-centered needs above meeting the needs of others.

As you strengthen and build qualities within yourself, you are then better able to make the right choices when choosing a spouse. God created us to admire and to love, but how we fulfill these desires, can, at times, be wrong. A spouse was not designed to fulfill all our needs; only God can fill the void. He or she was, however, designed to complement and to love the other. Marriage was intended to be a safe haven and a shelter; it was also designed to reflect our relationship with God, not take the place of it.

Marriage was intended to reflect our relationship with God, not take the place of it.

God revealed areas in my own life that needed improvement as I was praying for a godly wife. I would often think, "I'll work on those character flaws, but in the meantime, I want . . ." My attitude was wrong. *He wanted my priority to first be self-improvement rather than self-fulfillment.* It's acceptable to pray for what we want with right motives, but we also need to pray that God will mold us into the person He wants us to be—who we are is often who we will attract.

Who we are is often who we will attract.

THERE IS HOPE—A STRUGGLE VS. LIFESTYLE

How can we tell if we're struggling with sin or if it has become a lifestyle? Bishop T.D. Jakes offers an excellent analogy in a series entitled *I'll Never Do That Again—The Temptation Series, 2002*. He makes the comparison of a pig and a lamb that both find their way to the mud. The mud represents the sin that all of us fall into from time to time. The pig, the person who has made sin a lifestyle, wallows in the mud and enjoys it. The lamb, the believer who struggles with sin, hates the mud and cries when he or she is stuck. That's the difference. Do you jump in and wallow around, or do you feel remorse and conviction when you step in? Again, the flesh and the spirit are constantly at war, and our choices are never free from this battle. Romans 7:25 also recognizes this struggle ". . . with the mind I myself serve the law of God, but with the flesh the law of sin." To change a lifestyle, one must apply biblical truths and avoid sinful distractions.

As a word of support, it's never too late for a new beginning. Throughout the Old Testament God continually called His people back to Him. The only command Jesus gave the woman caught in the act of adultery was *to go and sin no more* (John 8:11). He didn't condemn her, criticize her or bring up the past; He gave her clear direction concerning what to do from that point forward. Yes, there are consequences for past mistakes, but it's best to find yourself in God's arms redeemed, then to live broken outside of His will. Which way will you run?

It's best to find yourself in God's arms redeemed, then to live broken outside of His will.

QUESTIONS TO CONSIDER:

When Michelle separated herself from God's presence, and from His protection, she had two choices, to fall backward or to fall forward. How could she have *fallen forward?*

We're often too smart to take large, deliberate plunges, but we can be enticed to take one step at a time, one compromise at a time, until it's too late. Are there areas in your life that are taking you down? If so, how can you break free?

(For men) We are called to be the spiritual leaders in the relationship. In what ways can you begin, or continue to fulfill this role?

In general, are you positioned to be drawn away by the strong pull of sin, or are you firmly footed on solid ground? In what areas do you need solid footing?

How can you continually build and strengthen your faith?

Memorize Isaiah 7:9, ". . . If you do not stand firm in your faith, you will not stand at all" (NIV).

It has been wisely stated that if you want to assess your priorities, simply review your checkbook and calendar.

CHAPTER SIX

Principle

Prioritizing

First things first

DON'T OVERLOOK A WEAK FOUNDATION BECAUSE YOU LIKE THE VIEW

My father was known in our valley for his ability to understand the lay of the land, the condition of the soil and water tables; landowners would sometimes consult him before building. Several rural communities nestled in the foothills near our home were developed around small lakes, and thus, on very high water tables and unstable ground. My father understood the desire to have a lakeside view, but he would often comment about his concern for residents who chose to buy or build a home on questionable ground because of view and location. In time, several families were forced to relocate due to rising water levels. The cost to repair or maintain these homes would sometimes cost thousands of dollars.

Stable ground is also essential in developing a positive relationship. As mentioned in the first chapter, the structure of marriage today is challenged because, in general, the foundation is weak. For example, a spouse may find that after a year of marriage her husband has had an affair. His problem with infidelity stemmed from a weak foundation. Did she choose a person of character? Did he demonstrate integrity? Did he have positive role models in his life? Did he seek God wholeheartedly? These are questions to ask before marriage. Unfortunately, *many overlook a weak foundation because they like the view.* Singles often overlook major character flaws because they like how the person looks or makes them feel. It's primarily the foundation (character) not the view (looks) alone that determines success or failure in a marriage, especially through adversity. The inner qualities of a gracious heart are enduring but outer beauty is fleeting. Take away the body and what do you have? In time, that body will change and hopefully you'll be happy with the person inside.

> *The foundation (character) not the view (external looks), determines success or failure in a marriage.*

In Matthew 7:25, Jesus states "and the rain descended, the floods came, and the winds blew and beat on that house; and it did not fall, for it was founded on the rock." The wise man, the man who built his house on the solid rock of Christ rather than on the shifting sand of man's philosophy, withstood the storm, but the foolish man who did not build his house on solid ground lost everything (Matthew 7:27). Strive to build character rich in patience, trust, love, perseverance, commitment and godly wisdom; God will provide plenty of opportunity through experience to develop these qualities. It's important to see challenges as opportunities for growth and it's equally important to find someone who is working to develop these same qualities. Remember, both men encountered a storm. Adversity comes to all of us. Build expecting storms, (especially in marriage) and recognize that you can weather them successfully through application of godly principles and a trusting attitude under the direction of the Holy Spirit.

If you're un-fulfilled as a single, the problem may be that you haven't applied fundamental principles to your life. When external pressures of life exceed internal strengths, our lives can easily collapse. For example, others may be pressuring you to marry, your biological clock is ticking, you're tired of being alone or perhaps, it's a combination of all three. Being single isn't about living life on hold until we meet someone—it's about living life to the fullest even if we don't. Whether you're attending college, pursuing a career and/or serving others, the time while single is invaluable. Yes, there are occasions when we feel lonely and want a partner, but those feelings should not control our lives. During my single years, I longed for a female companion, but tried not to live my life on hold. I wrote my first book, half of this one, started three other titles and developed WhyDietsDontWork.com, all while single. In addition, I studied the Bible regularly, listened to countless hours of sermons, read nearly forty books and worked from time to time with my brother's construction company. With out a shadow of doubt, it was a very productive time of my life. 1 Corinthians 7:32–33 (NLT) states that ". . . An unmarried man can spend his time doing the Lord's work and thinking how to please Him. But a married man can't do that so well. He has to think about his earthly responsibilities and how to please his wife." We shouldn't view singleness as a burden but a blessing—being single can allow us to accomplish more in other areas, not less.

> *Being single isn't about living life on hold until we meet someone—it's about living life to the fullest even if we don't.*

> *We shouldn't view singleness as a burden but a blessing.*

First priorities should be those things that build godly character (e.g., Bible reading, serving others, praying and associating with those who seek to maintain spiritual standards). At times, challenges are God sent; at other times, they may be the direct result of sin or a violation of spiritual principles. Determine where you turned left instead of right. From time to time you may not know why certain challenges arise, they may simply be opportunities for growth. Trust and obedience will help you stay on course during those times when nothing seems clear; simply continue to put first things first.

THE NUMBER ONE EXCUSE

Time is the number one excuse for those who don't exercise or eat properly. Ironically, time is also the number one excuse that keeps us from putting first things first. How often have we said or heard others say that they don't have enough time in their day to do this or that? I want to challenge those, who like myself, do have time to put first things first. We often forget just how precious time is. How many weeks, months or even years do we waste because we don't prioritize our lives? We need to be very careful when we say that we don't have enough time, because what we are sometimes saying is that it's not important enough.

I'm amazed at how many men "don't have time" for their family, but find time to play golf, watch television, pursue their hobbies or go out with friends. I've fallen into this trap myself and I've noticed that the real issue isn't time, but rather how we choose to spend it. If the average American family has television on seven hours a day, it's safe to assume that an individual can easily watch at least two hours a day or sixty hours a month. The need to put first things first has never been greater. As stated earlier, if we don't schedule time, time will schedule us.

> *If we don't schedule time, time will schedule us.*

Time is not like money; it can't be earned, borrowed or saved. You do, however, spend it, so spend wisely.

In essence, success is about leading a productive, balanced life, using time wisely. Desire will find a way, but excuses will hide it; therefore, it's important to get rid of excuses and prioritize your day. Ask yourself, "What's the most important thing for me to do in any given hour?" For example, contrary to what many think, reading the Bible and praying actually helps with the utilization of time. They aid in the area of discipline, patience,

> *Desire will find a way, but excuses will hide it.*

peace, joy and self-esteem. I've also found that it seems that my time, like money, is multiplied when I give first to God. Social life, business life and personal life all benefit from making spiritual growth a priority. I've found that if I'm too busy to pray or read the Bible—I'm too busy!

Prioritizing means putting first things first. Consider finances; tithing is crucial, but sometimes difficult. Developing strong relationships with family is crucial, but sometimes difficult. Getting and staying fit is crucial, but sometimes difficult. This shouldn't surprise us, Proverbs 14:23 states, "In all labor there is profit, but idle chatter leads only to poverty." Labor is another word for *effort;* idle is another word for *inactivity.* In simpler terms, effort produces results; inactivity doesn't! Putting first things first leads to success because those things in life worth having generally take energy and commitment to achieve.

PRINCIPLE SIX:

PRIORITIZING

All this talk about priorities, discipline, perseverance, commitment and making wise choices can be overwhelming, but you will find that they will actually increase your sense of control and overall well-being. Take small steps, and focus on the goal of character development rather than on the process of change.

OUR FIRST PRIORITY—IT MAY SURPRISE YOU

When I began dating Morgan, I recognized the need to exercise love the way God, not society, defines it. I needed to work on patience, kindness and serving, and to begin to trust, believe in her and to protect her. This didn't mean that I was to ignore red flags, but *there's a difference between red flags and workable issues.* For example, once Morgan and I worked through the initial stages of courting and felt good about moving forward, my role was to love her regardless of her emotional struggles. Love doesn't say, "That's your problem, deal with"; it says,

We'll never find the perfect person, but we can find the perfect person for us.

"How can I help you in this area?" *Love is a choice, not a feeling.* We'll never find the perfect person, but with God's help, we'll find the perfect person for us.

Determine if your concern is a valid red flag or simply an issue to work through. Can you work through this problem together and with counsel, or does it need to be dealt with individually? If the problem places tremendous strain on the relationship, it may be wise to postpone a serious relationship— it largely depends on the individual and the circumstance. If you notice red flags while dating, such as substance abuse, violence, chronic dishonesty, cheating and/or problems with uncontrolled lust, for example, it's probably time to end the relationship.

Ultimately, *God knows your heart when you fall short.* This is the one final thought that I find most helpful in dealing with my own issues and disappointments. Rather than continuing to badger yourself with guilt, simply state "Lord you know my heart, help me"; then let it go.

Now back on course . . . how should we love? No, this isn't a trick question. If love is the greatest commandment, it should be our first priority. When our view of love is misunderstood, we get into trouble. For example, attraction is not love, it's simply attraction—*a pull toward a particular person or thing.*

> *If love is the greatest commandment, it should be our first priority.*

Countless couples say that they are in love when, in reality, they are attracted. Attraction comes and goes, but true love was created to endure. Most would agree, however, that attraction is initially what draws us together. Ideally, attraction continues throughout marriage, however the spiritual essence of love gives it holding power.

The Bible defines love, *"Love is patient, love is kind. It does not envy, it does not boast, it is not proud. It is not rude, it is not self-seeking, it is not easily angered, it keeps no record of wrongs. Love does not delight in evil but rejoices with the truth. It always protects, always trusts, always hopes, always perseveres"* (1 Corinthians 13:4–7 NIV). This is how we are to love . . . our spouses, our friends, our children and so on.

LOVE IS PATIENT, LOVE IS KIND

We should be patient and understanding with the needs of others. This could simply mean being patient as your partner takes twice as long as you to get ready to go, or it may require more patience as they work through their weaknesses. Patience means taking time to be supportive and understanding, and not allowing our needs to get in the way of their needs. There are times, however, when you may need to talk to your partner when his or her requests or expectations seem unreasonable. Reserve a night to share what's on your minds, in a non-threatening manner. Both should allow the other to talk with no interruptions. Truly listen and try to understand the other's needs. There is wise counsel in the words, *seek first to understand and then to be understood.* Repeat back what is said to make sure that what is said is what is heard. We're often misunderstood and we sometimes fail to meet the need of another for a practical reason rather than a selfish motive.

LOVE DOES NOT ENVY OR BOAST, NOR IS IT PROUD . . .

When the spirit of envy enters our heart, it's difficult to love the way God intended. In the marriage relationship, *envy or jealousy can occur when couples view their relationship as competition rather than a commitment to cooperate.* This can happen when two people are actively involved together in ministry, school or careers. If not careful, they may compete with one another rather than pursue their goals together. Encourage the success of one another as well as the success of the relationship.

KEEP NO RECORD OF WRONG, NOR DELIGHT IN EVIL

Relationships are like checking accounts. Words of healing and praise are deposits into our emotional bank account; words of anger and insults are withdrawals. If there are more withdrawals than deposits, the account not only loses value but it can create emotional bankruptcy. Emotional bankruptcy happens frequently in relationships, especially marriage. Learn to make deposits and avoid withdrawals if you want the highest yield from your relationship. We're human and, from time to time, we say and do things that hurt others. Others say and do things that hurt us. God instructs us to overlook the wrongs done against us, and hopefully others will do the same; keep the account open. (I'm not referring to allowing chronic physical, emotional or verbal abuse. If you are dating and this is a problem, stop! If you are married, seek help from those who will give scriptural counsel, and never underestimate the power of prayer.)

Sometimes we attack one another with our words, and although done in humor, words carry enormous weight. If a wife is continually called lazy or bothersome, her self-esteem will eventually deteriorate and the relationship will lose its value. One very common, indirect insult is to ask your spouse what he or she has done all day. The Bible directs us to ". . . be slow to speak . . ." (James 1:19). God wants us to think before we speak and/or respond.

LOVE ALWAYS HOPES, TRUSTS, PROTECTS AND PERSEVERES

Hope means to anticipate, expect or to look forward to something. Love hopes for and believes the best in others. It is translated through our actions and our words. We may not always see the best in others, but we trust that it is there and we encourage it to grow.

We may not always see the best in others, but we trust that it is there and we encourage it to grow.

We want to develop the type of love that protects, defends and guards the self-esteem and integrity of others.

Finally, perseverance is the principle that holds us together. It is the "stick-to-it-iveness" that binds us together during hard times. As mentioned earlier, studies indicate that couples who reported being unhappy, when interviewed years later, reported being happy, and very pleased that they remained together.

Let me take the opportunity, at this point, to address the harm in living together before marriage. The cultural concept of living together does not allow for perseverance. In essence, it states that there is no need to work through difficult challenges because there is no solid commitment. Without a commitment to "work-through", individuals can move from relationship to relationship and never allow time to develop a strong union. Working through challenges is the very ingredient that builds lasting relationships.

Couples today often want the freedom to divorce and leave the marriage if it doesn't work out; marriage never works out, you have to work it out. Living together fails to offer this most important factor, and thus, defeats itself.

Marriage never works out, you have to work it out.

True love is first a commitment to another to be patient, kind and to serve, despite emotional highs and lows. Make love your top priority—it will not rise to that level left alone.

Make love your top priority—it will not rise to that level left alone.

PRIORITIZING

In your journal, develop a list of priorities, and arrange your schedule within this framework. Briefly list your top priorities such as spiritual growth, family, health and career. List also what you feel they should be.

EXAMPLE:

Date: _____

What they are currently	What my top priorities should be:
1. _____	1. _____
2. _____	2. _____
3. _____	3. _____
4. _____	4. _____
5. _____	5. _____

And so on . . .

What immediate changes can you make to correct your current order? In thirty days, list your priorities again and compare with those you established thirty days prior.

QUESTIONS TO CONSIDER:

Before marriage, ask questions such as, does my potential spouse demonstrate integrity? Does he or she have positive role models? Does he or she seek God wholeheartedly? If not, how might this damage the relationship in the future?

If dating, ask this question, "If you take away the body, what do you have?"

Being single isn't about living life on hold until we meet someone, it's about living life to the fullest even if we don't. If you haven't already, how can you begin living life to the fullest? What would you like to pursue?

Are you scheduling time, or is time scheduling you?

Do you agree that love should be your first priority?

Memorize 1 Corinthians 13:4–7, "Love is patient, love is kind. It does not envy, it does not boast, it is not proud. It is not rude, it is not self-seeking, it is not easily angered, it keeps no record of wrongs. Love does not delight in evil but rejoices with the truth. It always protects, always trusts, always hopes, always perseveres" (NIV). (Try replacing the word love with your name; how are you doing?)

. . . and the lectures you deliver may be very wise and true; But I'd rather get my lesson by observing what you do. For I may misunderstand you and the high advice you give, But there's no misunderstanding how you act and how you live.

—Edgar A. Guest
"Sermons we see" from the book, The Light of Faith.

CHAPTER SEVEN

Principle

Character

---

*Character—a lifetime to build,
seconds to destroy*

WHEN A VESSEL IS STRUCK, WHAT'S INSIDE SPILLS OUT

I remember a news story involving an enormous oil tanker that sprung a leak off the coast of Spain and millions of gallons of oil gushed out into the sea. It was a horrific site and an environmental disaster. The oil tanker was defenseless against the spill because it was full of oil. In the same way, when an individual is struck, what's inside spills out. Is anger, pride or selfishness exposed, or does adversity reveal patience, forgiveness, commitment, peace, and/or perseverance? *The next time your vessel is struck, consider a cargo check!*

Regrettably, character appears to be losing ground largely because today's culture often runs contrary to spiritual values. Again, Galatians 5:17 (NLT) describes this conflict, ". . . And the spirit gives us desires that are opposite from what the sinful nature desires. These two forces are constantly fighting each other, and your choices are never free from this conflict." Clearly, the battle is for our spiritual character. Commit the battle to Christ, and incorporate the A,B,C,'s of spiritual warfare.

A,B,C,'s of Developing a Godly Response

Acknowledge the warfare.   Ephesians 6:12 reminds us, "For we do not wrestle against flesh and blood, but against principalities, against powers, against the rulers of the darkness of this age, against spiritual hosts of wickedness in the heavenly places." Acknowledge simply means to recognize. If we don't recognize that there is a thief determined to steal, to kill and to destroy, we won't be prepared to defend or to counterattack.

> *"The thief does not come except to steal, and to kill, and to destroy. I have come that they may have life, and that they may have it more abundantly."*
> —John 10:10

Be prepared.   Armies that are undefeated are well prepared. Companies that survive fluctuating economies are prepared. Successful marriages are prepared. Preparation simply means to be ready for the challenges ahead. Olympic athletes spend years preparing for one event. In the same way, we should spend time preparing for the unforeseen challenges ahead. Remember, we play like we practice.

How do we prepare? Romans 12:2 states, "And do not be conformed to this world, but be transformed by the renewing of your mind . . ." Conform means to do the acceptable thing. In order to be accepted by society, many of us conform to its standards. When the Apostle Paul said, ". . . be transformed by the renewing of your mind," he was advising us to change and renew our thinking, and thus, our actions. Scripture helps us to discern our deepest thoughts and intentions: "For the word of God is living and powerful, and sharper than any two-edge sword, piercing even to the division of soul and spirit, and of joints and marrow, and is a discerner of the thoughts and intents of the heart" (Hebrews 5:12). Scripture is intensely powerful; it brings to light those areas of darkness within us, and allows us to see if we are otherwise minded; in short, it exposes who we really are. Discipline yourself to continue to pray and read, even if you don't see the immediate results you had hoped for—you will. Remember . . . *He is a rewarder of those who diligently seek Him* (Hebrews 11:6).

> *He is a rewarder of those who diligently seek Him.*
> —Hebrews 11:6

The enemy would like us to believe that prayer is ineffective and that serving Christ is not rewarding. Preparation involves being obedient in doing what is right even though there appears to be no outward evidence of results.

Continually hold your ground. Many of our battles will be ongoing because we were born into a sinful world. Don't let this discourage you, ". . . greater is He who is in you than he who is in the world" (1 John 4:4 NASB). Forces within our minds are constantly battling and we are never totally free from this conflict, but we can defend against attack with the Word of God. Again, our thoughts become our words, our words become actions, actions form habits and habits shape our character. Paul provides additional answers in Philippians 4:8 (NLT): ". . . Fix your thoughts on what is true and honorable and right. Think about things that are pure and lovely and admirable. Think about things that are excellent and worthy of praise." Additionally, he states, "For though we walk in the flesh, we do not war according to the flesh. For the weapons of our warfare are not carnal but mighty in God for pulling down strongholds, casting down arguments and every high thing that exalts itself against the knowledge of God, *bringing every thought into captivity to the obedience of Christ*" (II Corinthians 10:3–5—italics mine). Paul understood, as should we, that good thoughts will eventually produce good actions. And, when our vessel is struck, godly character will come forth.

> *Good thoughts will eventually produce good actions.*

Yesterday's Seeds, Tomorrow's Harvest

Many of our nation's founders and early leaders were men of character. They recognized spiritual principles fundamental for ". . . life, liberty and the pursuit of happiness."

I'm a firm believer that *if we don't water the roots the plants will die.* I grew up in Southern California and was trained by a mother who had a passion for seasonal flowers and chore charts. My job one summer, in addition to others, was watering the flowerpots that lined our front and back patios. It was a simple job, but I was easily bored and anxious to get on with other things. After quickly sprinkling the plants for several days, most of the flowers withered and died. Rather than a lecture, mom felt that the best way to teach responsibility and the need to soak the roots, was to have me replace the flowers from my allowance. I learned a valuable lesson: *keep the roots alive.* In the same way, if we fail to keep America's spiritual roots alive we may lose a rich harvest of God's blessing and the cost will be great.

Nearly four-hundred years ago, English Puritans set sail for a land where God's ordinances would govern, and America was born. At that time, our Founding Fathers understood the wisdom in God's directives for a prosperous life. In William Martin's book, *A Prophet with Honor-The Billy Graham Story,* he recalls John Cotton's warning to the Puritans . . . "as soon as God's Ordinances cease, your Security ceaseth likewise; but if God plant his Ordinances among you, fear not, he will maintain them." In other words, when we fail to cultivate God's Word, our security, defense and protection can cease, yet God will continue to call from each generation those who will support His laws (i.e., ordinances); I believe that we, you and I, are called in this generation to support these truths.

> *You and I, are called in this generation to support these truths.*

Our country's motto has been "In God we Trust," and our national mindset reflected Christian values. Sadly enough, today's culture promotes *relativism* and man does what is right in his own eyes—abortion and divorce are now determined by personal preference rather than by God's Word. Pornography is commonly protected as an expression of free speech, while school prayer is often banned. Our society clearly reflects man's digression from God; our nation's current culture cannot produce safe, secure living. Fortunately, for those who follow Christ, He promises peace amidst the chaos.

Where do you stand on abortion, sexual abstinence, honesty, commitment and respect for others? Do you accept the secular philosophy that what feels right is right, or do you follow spiritual directives? For those who may be skeptical, let me present one question: if the Bible is the Word of God, and if moral absolutes were given to guide, direct and protect mankind, where will the enemy attack? You got it . . . in the realm of moral absolutes.

As previously mentioned, America's present philosophy of relativism/secular humanism runs contrary to God's wisdom and is spreading throughout education, government and the justice system, largely by those who were educated by this philosophy in the 1960's and somewhat earlier. Those schooled by secular humanism have greatly influenced legislation and cultural values. The transition from God-centered principles to man-centered values is a spiritual war deliberately waged by the adversary.

There was a time in our recent history when America felt secure knowing that its most formidable enemies were abroad. Today, our nation is threatened by relentless enemies both foreign and within. I'm reminded of the story of a young girl who wrote this letter: "Dear God, why did You allow armed students to walk into a school and open fire on the students?" He replied, *"Dear little girl, because I'm no longer allowed in schools."* Removing God from our country is as tragic as removing Him from our schools. It is sobering to think that today's students will be tomorrow's leaders. Fortunately, there are young people rising who are passionate about personal and national integrity based on absolutes. If this is you, I encourage you to continue; you will make a difference!

When we remove God, we remove His covering and protection. As a nation, II Chronicles 7:14 provides direction, we are to humble ourselves, pray, seek God and turn from our sinful ways (paraphrased). Clearly, *the prayer that we pray today may be the tragedy that we avert tomorrow.*

> *The prayer that we pray today may be the tragedy that we avert tomorrow.*

As I was concluding this chapter, I heard a news commentator discuss terrorist activity and how we can prepare for future attacks. The commentator then turned attention to the problem in corporate America; he stated that Americans are losing trust in large companies because of inflated profit margins and lack of ethical principles. It struck me that while we are concerned with terrorist attacks, and rightly so, there is a greater threat from corruption within. America's blessings are simply the fruit of yesterday's past. There is a saying: *one generation plants trees for the next generation.* I am concerned that, rather than planting, we are tearing them down and removing the very covering that protects us.

> *America's blessings are simply the fruit of yesterday's past.*

I say all that to say this, as Christians, we are called to lead our families, our communities and our nation within a framework of spiritual principles. We are directed to hold fast to our commitments, to our integrity and to our values. Don't be fooled by thinking you can't make a difference—you can; society changes as individuals change. We are to believe in God, accept His Son, exhibit faith and walk with integrity. M.H. McKee states it well, "Integrity is one of several paths. It distinguishes itself from the others because it is the right path, and the only one upon which you will never get lost."

> *Society changes as individuals change.*

The book of Job gives a biblical account of a man who lost everything, his children, his home and his livelihood in an effort, by the enemy, to challenge his beliefs and ultimately destroy his character. In time, God restored Job's wealth, and more, because he held fast to his integrity. Are you holding on to your integrity? If not, you can change that today.

If we look to the world for guidance and direction, our foundation as singles and as married couples stands on very shaky ground. Application of God's principles builds, restores and provides stability for positive relationships, whether single or married. As an individual, honesty and commitment to spiritual values are the most important asset that you bring into the relationship.

KNOWING GOD'S WILL

The Character Test

There are far greater books written on knowing the will of God than what I can express in a few short pages. Authors such as Jack Hayford, Charles Stanley, Josh McDowell, James Dobson, and Chuck Swindoll, to name only a few, have written exceptional books on the subject.

The following pages will not outline God's specific will for your life, however, they will outline certain principles and truths that provide guidance for the journey.

Whether single, dating or married, knowing the will of God is a desire we all have. Unfortunately, many focus on the external circumstances of life and not on the inner condition of the heart. We may live in a certain location, have the job we want and be married to the person of our choice, but often, many of our plans don't produce the peace or fulfillment that we had hoped for, largely because we don't align our will with God's. We want what we think will make us happy—God wants to develop our character and prepare us for an eternal reward. Although topics such as marriage and career are important to address, they don't supercede our need to address character development. For instance, God's will for my life is centered less on the *WHAT WORKS Book Series* and more on who I am as a person. The Scripture, ". . . A life of moral excellence leads to knowing God better" (II Peter 1:5 NLT), assures us that one of the best ways to know God's plans is to live life morally upright.

Many focus on the external circumstances of life and not on the inner condition of the heart.

We want what we think will make us happy—God wants to develop our character.

The Bible often illustrates the fact that God is working on character rather than on superficial things. In the Old Testament, for example, God gave many the opportunity to be leaders, and it was character, not position, that determined outcome. *Determining God's will for our lives should first center on developing godly attributes rather than reaching a goal.*

> *It was character, not position, that determined outcome.*

When we are walking in obedience to God's Word, many times, the struggles that we encounter are not an indicator that we are out of God's will but rather that He is molding us into His image, or they are part of a unfolding plan. Mary and Joseph could easily have questioned God's will when Mary, pregnant and ready to deliver, rode on a donkey to an unfamiliar town only to find that there was no room for her to lodge and to give birth.

Instead of asking, "What is God's will for my life?" We should be asking, "How can I develop and strengthen my character while pursuing His will?"

Our Ability Will Only Take Us As Far As Our Character Will Allow Us to Go

Reputation is who we are around others; character is who we are when others aren't around. It's been said that you can tell cowards from heroes by which way they run. In the same way, character is the most powerful tool in transmitting to others who we are and what we stand for. America has some of the most talented athletes and entrepreneurs in the world, but *ability will only take them as far as their character will allow them to go.* You may climb the ladder of success, but it's your character that will keep you at the top.

> *Reputation is who we are around others; character is who we are when others aren't around.*

Corporate America offers rich opportunity, and without profit, companies cease to exist, *but they need to be character-driven as well as production-driven.* Lately, we have witnessed the down-fall of corporations that lost the balance between profitability and accountability. Character traits such as integrity, honesty, loyalty and trust were somehow removed from company policy. The Bible tells us that we are to profit or yield a return in what we do, but it also clarifies that we are to do it honestly and with correct motives.

It takes time to develop godly character; don't get discouraged. Although good character is a matter of choice, it is also forged through affliction and tempered by adversity; it is built through the challenges we face and the obstacles we overcome.

Godly character can rebuild a marriage, restore a relationship and influence others to follow its lead. In contrast, bad character can ruin a marriage, destroy a relationship and

PRINCIPLE SEVEN:

CHARACTER

draw the wrong crowd. Words, choices and habits all reflect character. The first step in seeking God's will is to develop godly character and to allow Him to direct your steps— "The steps of a good man are ordered by the Lord . . ." (Psalm 37:23).

The Real Meaning of Boot Camp

Since recommitting my life to Christ, one of my prayers has been to continually focus on character development, but I had no idea what I was asking. Imagine a man entering the Marine Corps; he knows he wants to be a Marine but has no idea what to expect. The first day he is awe-struck by what's required of him, but the countless hours of training, the ongoing testing and the discipline to remain committed eventually pay off and he graduates a Marine. Was the process easy? Hardly! It was the most difficult training he'd ever faced. One doesn't merely attend boot camp for a few days, take a test and go home; the process is rigorous and intense. Likewise, when God develops character, He does so to meet the challenges ahead and to prepare us for life. We too are tested, trained and disciplined, but the rewards far outweigh the process. How do we develop patience if we're not tested? How do we develop forgiveness if we are never wronged? How do we learn to trust God if we're never in need? *Trying times are often intended to build us up not to break us down.* James 1:2–4 states, "My brethren, count it all joy when you fall into various trials, knowing that the testing of your faith produces

> *Trying times are often intended to build us up not break us down.*

patience. But let patience have its perfect work, that you may be perfect and complete, lacking nothing." Focus on character more than comfort and you'll be happy with the outcome.

How well do you hear?

Many times, we have the order reversed; we want to hear from God and then we'll work on our character. *God tells us to work on character and then we'll be better able to hear.*

Keys to Hearing Clearly

➤ **Recognize that God's will, unless it is written, is not as clearly defined as a road map.** "Should I turn left or right?" "Should I work on a paper or exercise?" "Should I sleep in or get up?" The "should I's" can be endless. God's will is a journey as well as a destination. God told Abraham in Genesis 12:1, ". . . go to the land that I will show you" (NLT). So it is with us. He teaches us to sense His direction through the guidance of the Holy Spirit, and to move accordingly. Sometimes we do experience a true sense of God's exact direction, but often, we simply walk by faith. If you feel that God is leading you and if the leading does not run contrary to His Word, move forward even if it seems unclear at times. Generally, it's simply a matter of acknowledging Proverbs 3:6 . . . commit your ways to Him daily, trusting that He is directing your path (paraphrased).

God's will is a journey as well as a destination.

➤ **Compare what you're feeling to the Word of God.** How often do we sense a stirring in our spirit and are not sure if it's God or not, especially when dating? A good question to ask is, "Am I following my flesh or God?" Attraction is important, but if attraction is the only thing that holds a couple together, it's going to be a difficult journey. Remember, God's will always corresponds with His Word. For example, contrary to God's Word, many Christians date and marry unbelievers. Regardless of feelings, God's Word does not change. Does this mean that God cannot bless Christians if they've married unbelievers? No, but being equally yoked is not just a good idea; it is God's principle intended to promote the health of the relationship. The more we ignore God's leading, the

Being equally yoked is not just a good idea; it is God's principle intended to promote the health of the relationship.

harder it becomes to hear His voice; we can become spiritually deaf. Again, compare your direction to Scripture. Does it line up? If you are dating and sense that you're in a wrong relationship, step away and take time to analyze; you can't go wrong by waiting for direction.

➤ **Accept the assignment.** This is difficult for me because I like telling God what to do. For example, when I felt the overwhelming sense to sell my home, I knew that God was leading me away from Corporate America and into the unknown, but I fought the urge to sell. I thought, "Surely God will allow me to keep my home," but eventually I put it on the market. I hoped it wouldn't sell, but it did. Within three weeks I had an offer. At the last minute I backed out, still believing that God wanted me to own the home that I designed and built. During the months that followed, the desire to leave my career was greater than ever, and I knew that I needed to sell my house. In a rush, I contacted a real-estate agent and sold it within a few months. However, I received thousands of dollars less than I would have received initially had I listened and heeded His voice. When we hear from God, we need to respond in faith. God is not playing games like "Do this", "No, I mean do that", "No, do this again." The key is to heed the *correct* voice and move forward. I felt that my initial thought was the correct leading because it was the wise thing to do—I needed to save money more than I needed a new home. Was it easy at first? No, but the weeks that followed brought tremendous comfort.

➤ **Patiently and quietly listen.** When I first felt the need to sell my home, I prayed about it and patiently waited. My desire to sell continued to grow and many godly people confirmed the decision because it was the wise thing to do. Many of us lead very busy lives, which makes it difficult to be in the right frame of mind to hear from God. It wasn't until I spent each morning in solitude and prayer that I began to sense direction. As I read, and prayed, and fasted occasionally, His will began to unfold. From my experience, I found that God doesn't always say yes or no immediately, he tells us to wait and be patient. His leading isn't a thoughtless course of action; it's a well-designed plan that requires patience, and patience builds character. On another note, it's incredibly difficult to hear God if we're actively engaging in sin. Sin means to *miss the mark*—we can't be on target, in the center of God's will, if we're missing the mark.

➤ **Keep moving.** You might ask, "If we are to patiently wait and quietly listen, how can we keep moving?" Although there are clearly times when God wants us to wait, it's difficult to direct what's not moving. During my childhood and teen years, my family often vacationed and fished in the Eastern Sierra Nevada Mountain Range near June Lake, California. Once on the lake, Dad would accelerate the boat motor and head off until we reached our destination. He would then turn off the motor and lower the anchor. On one occasion (when I was very young), after the motor was stilled and we began fishing, I tried steering the boat. No matter which direction I turned the wheel, the boat stood still. I asked my dad why the boat wasn't working. He said that it was working but that it could not be directed unless it was moving. In the same way, God may be directing us, but if we're not moving, we won't get anywhere. Moving doesn't mean walking around without an agenda, it means serving God and others, living life to the fullest and doing our best each and every day. For those single, when God brings a spouse, it's often when we're moving in the right direction, not looking in the wrong direction.

When God brings a spouse, it's often when we're moving in the right direction, not looking in the wrong direction.

➤ **His will is often revealed over time.** Most of us want immediate answers when we seek direction, but more often than not, if it's not written, God's will tends to be a process rather than an instant revelation. Granted, there are times when the Holy Spirit directs us instantly—prompting a phone call to a friend in need, or leading us to make a quick decision, but we usually see only portions of the big picture. When I felt an inner sense directing me to leave an eight-year profession, I only saw glimpses of the big picture. It seemed unlikely, but I envisioned myself writing books, hosting seminars and promoting *Christian* values. I had no idea how it would unfold. God asks us to walk in faith and trust Him.

God's will tends to be a process rather than an instant revelation.

➤ **Don't be surprised by challenges.** I once believed that life was easy while in the center of God's will and if life wasn't easy, I was out of His will. This is not always true. Yes, we should have peace in the center of God's will, but at times we may fight bouts of anxiety, depression and fear. Many biblical heroes fought hardship and anxiety while being in the center of God's will. Abraham, Sarah, Joseph, Moses, Elijah, Esther, Jeremiah, Isaiah, Mary, the Apostle Paul, the Disciples all faced difficult times and challenging circumstances. When I finished writing *WHAT WORKS When "Diets" Don't,* I experienced periods of anxiety and depression. Was this an indicator that I was out of God's will? Of course not— His will was in process. I trusted Him, kept moving forward and continued working toward my goals. Was it easy? No, but within a few months, new opportunities arose . . . I had been praying for a spouse for a few years and it looked as if God was answering my prayer, but three months into my relationship with Morgan, anxiety and fear overwhelmed me again. Were we out of God's will? At the time, we both believed that we were. We separated to step back from the relationship and to seek clear direction. Being apart didn't confirm that the relationship should end, and we began to date again. How did we determine if we were in God's will? First, we focused on God's moral will for our lives through purity and honesty. Second, we focused on obeying His Word and His principles. Third, we sought counsel and used wisdom, and relied on God to guide us. Was it trouble-free? Not at all. Divorce had made me fearful of starting again, and Morgan's issues with self-esteem continued to contribute to her anxiety—this is the "personal baggage" you often hear referred to. "Extra baggage" does not make the journey wrong—it simply means there's more to carry.

> *"Extra baggage" does not make the journey wrong—it simply means there's more to carry.*

Unquestionably, being in the center of God's will does not prevent challenges; sometimes it creates them. As long as we were following His direction, walking morally upright and obeying His principles, we felt confident that He would direct us—one way or the other. And He will do the same for you.

➢ **God's will is always what's best for you.** I remember, as a teen, feeling that when I committed my life to Christ all the fun would be over and God might send me to a mission field in Uganda, for example. You probably know people who feel this way—maybe that's you. Nothing could be farther from the truth; God's will is always what is best for you although it may not feel like it from time to time. He's placed godly desires within you, and those desires will manifest themselves as you pursue His will. Missionaries will often tell you that they had a deep desire to serve God as a missionary. Many Christian businessmen and professionals also say they too felt inclined toward their specific field. God does not give talent and interests to be wasted; He encourages the desires of your heart as you seek to serve Him and others—God is the one who places the desire within you. (If you truly lack motivation and energy, consider a closer look at your overall health.)

➤ **His leading is generally calm and reassuring.** God seldom rushes us. Although there may be times when we must make a quick, timely decision, His will is generally calm and reassuring. If you feel rushed, stop and wait. If, for some reason, you can't wait, simply use wisdom and make the decision to the best of your ability. If you are seeking marriage, slow down, position yourself in God's will and wait on Him. You can rarely go wrong waiting, but you can often go wrong rushing.

You can rarely go wrong waiting, but you can often go wrong rushing.

THE SECRET TO SUCCESS

Most of us desire a happy marriage, a good life and great health. Unfortunately, desire alone is not enough. Any great feat began with someone's passionate action! Considering the number of people today who want a happy marriage, or a fulfilled life as a single—and that would be most—far too few actually arrive. Why? Many do not make an *ongoing* spiritual investment in a lifestyle that promotes healthy relationships.

In the past, marriage commitment was the factor that held the family together. It was in that setting that children learned, love grew and character developed. Divorce was rarely an option. In general, a husband or a wife was considered an asset, not a liability.

Today's high divorce rate is simply an indicator of how society has changed. I'm suggesting that we resurrect an attitude of service and commitment to the marriage relationship. People often say that they just need to get their lives together and then they'll do this or that. If this is you, don't wait to apply God's Word to your life—you may wait a lifetime. Start now,

Those who succeed walk through adversity, not without it.

regardless of your current situation. Those who succeed walk through adversity, not without it. There's no "best" time to start. Simply start now and remember that as long as you take two steps forward, even after stepping back, you'll continue to move in the right direction.

If one desires a successful marriage, he or she needs to be a committed spouse. If one desires a good job, he or she needs to be a good employee. If one desires a better relationship with his or her children, he or she needs to be a better parent. Despite what you might think, you do have the power to change. It's not the difficult circumstances of life that defeat us—but rather it is our attitude and response to circumstances that determines whether we succeed or fail.

It is our attitude and response to circumstances that determines whether we succeed or fail.

Anger, resentment, bitterness, failure, frustration and un-forgiveness can produce a negative, unproductive attitude! People that we surround ourselves with, and thoughts we entertain, will eventually be seen in our actions.

Life is like a race of endurance, full of endless opportunities and experiences. There are also occasional roadblocks, delays, pitfalls and hurdles. Make no mistake about it—*we win by persevering, by getting up and not giving in.* Successful people build success from failure, and they don't look back—it's not the direction they want to go. Focus on the goal, not the challenge, and move forward. Successful people often fail more than failures do; they simply refuse to give up.

Few things hurt us more than failing to forgive others or ourselves for past mistakes. Many times, memories haunt and discourage us from moving forward. As a result, people may rate themselves according to what they were, or what they did, not realizing that who they are and who they will become is far more important.

We live in a world that, often, will not allow us to forget our mistakes. There are too few people to encourage or help us along the way. People can either lift you up, or pull you down. If you're not sure if the person is a positive or negative influence, *consider where they are leading you;* is it the direction that you want to go? If not, reconsider the relationship.

In addition, avoid the "what others say and think" trap, unless it's positive. We often judge ourselves by their standards, failing to recognize that what people may say about us is not who we actually are. Don't let the opinions of others define you!

With life we were given power. The power to persevere is one of the greatest attributes that we possess. Learning from experience empowers us to move forward. There is little we can do about life's glitches except to control the way we respond to them. Remember, the obstacles ahead are not greater than God's power to take you through.

> *The obstacles ahead are not greater than God's power to take you through.*

Society tends to program our looks and actions. Women, as well as young girls, refer to magazines and TV to see how they should dress and act; teenage boys consult TV and the media for role models, and many men measure their self worth by what they have accomplished in business and financially, not realizing that a relationship with God, family and others is the treasure they should be seeking. It's little wonder that the family structure is rapidly declining.

Secular values have eroded qualities such as moral integrity, discipline and commitment from today's society, just as water and time have eroded the banks of the Colorado River and left a vast Grand Canyon. Erosion can occur so slowly that we are unaware until its work is done. It has the power to change the course of a mighty river and it can surely change the course of our lives. Don't allow a declining culture to erode essential qualities in your life.

In closing, the message of this book is simple and straightforward: life is often a reflection of the choices we make. Only a solid biblical foundation, along with a personal relationship with Jesus Christ, can provide solid direction in unstable times. Biblical principles simply help us *do what is right.* Wrong choices complicate your life and rob you of peace. With that in mind, is there really any choice?

Succeeding the way God designed it, whether married or single, is not difficult. Establish a goal and stay committed to Him. Control your thoughts, move forward and ignore setbacks. Prioritize your time, and stay motivated. Sound difficult? Not really. Most of us already do these things. We have goals, but perhaps they're wrong or un-realistic; we're committed, but sometimes to the wrong things; we have time, but it's frequently misappropriated; we have priorities, but they're sometimes misplaced; we feed our thoughts, but often with the wrong information; and we're disciplined, but only in certain areas of our lives . . . it's all about choosing wisely!

QUESTIONS TO CONSIDER:

The next time you're "struck", consider a cargo check. What areas need improvement?

Reputation is who you are around others; character is who you are when others aren't around. Should there be a difference?

Do you agree that if we neglect to water the roots of our Christian heritage, blessings may die? How can you make a difference?

We want what we think will make us happy—God wants to develop our character. Do you think happiness and character development go hand-in-hand?

How do you measure success?

Memorize James 1:2–4, "My brethren, count it all joy when you fall into various trials, knowing that the testing of your faith produces patience. But let patience have its perfect work, that you may be perfect and complete, lacking nothing."

You can't change where you've been, but you can change where you're going.

CHAPTER EIGHT

Divorce—Hope for the Hurting

Broken—yet unbreakable

TURNING BROKENNESS INTO AN UNBREAKABLE FORCE

In the book *Sacred Thirst,* published by Zondervan, Craig Barnes writes . . . "The bride and groom are standing in front of everyone, looking better than they are ever going to look again, getting so much attention and affirmation. Everybody even stands when they walk in so it's easy to think this marriage, at least, is about them. It's not. Just look at the worn-out parents sitting in the first pew—they understand this. The only reason these parents are still married is because long ago they learned how to handle the hurt they caused each other. *They know that the last thing you ever want to do with hurt is to let it define you"* (italics mine). This last statement offers one of the most profound points that I've read on brokenness. Those who do not allow hurt to entrap them can turn brokenness into an unbreakable force, but those shackled by past pain are truly imprisoned by it—the walls we build to protect us may eventually imprison us.

> *The walls we build to protect us may eventually imprison us.*

How can we undo the emotional pain we experience from failed relationships? First, understand that it's not an external fight—it's an internal struggle. Our minds are battlefields where personal conflicts are either won or lost. God works within our spirits by transmitting His Word into healthy thoughts. I don't mean to discount the deep emotional and psychological pain of failed relationships, but I do want to remind you that God makes provision for all of our needs.

Second, of all the books I've read, the sermons I've heard, the couples I've talked with and the devastation I've seen firsthand, one common denominator was present: *those who do not forgive or release bitterness, anger and hurt, never experience freedom, happiness or true restoration.* Ephesians 4:31-32 states . . . "Let all bitterness, wrath, anger, clamor, and evil speaking be put away from you, with all malice. And be kind to one another, tenderhearted, forgiving one another, even as God in Christ forgave you." Simply stated, if you fail to forgive, bitterness and anger, though skillfully masked, can and will tarnish future relationships. Divorced, separated or single, God can turn brokenness into an unbreakable force, but it is imperative that your mind is renewed by applying biblical principles, beginning with forgiveness.

With millions of American's now classified as divorced and "newly" single, the need to address this topic is unavoidable and necessary. For example, in 1998 over 19-million adults were estimated to be divorced. Those who have walked in true forgiveness know that God rebuilds if we are willing to grow. It's been well stated that pain can make us bitter or it can make us better.

Pain can make us bitter or it can make us better.

The word brokenness describes a variety of experiences. For the purpose of this section, we'll discuss brokenness of spirit. Brokenness resulting from the loss of a home, employment, money or other material possessions is much different from *relational* brokenness.

Years ago, I was listening to a syndicated Christian radio program during my morning run. A survivor of the holocaust was being interviewed. She described the horrific conditions of the concentration camps and then made a statement I'd never forget; *she described the emotional pain and the brokenness she experienced from her divorce as greater than the pain of the concentration camp.* Six months later, another guest on the same program, described the pain of losing her husband to cancer. She spoke about how his illness devastated their lives after ten long months of suffering. I was again moved to hear her say that she would have rather lost her husband to death by cancer than divorce. Unbelievable! Two different women who had gone through more pain than many of us will ever know said that divorce is, or would be, more painful than death. My mind searched for understanding . . . why was divorce more devastating than a concentration camp, or cancer? For several weeks I pondered this question. My answer came: death is a natural process and God makes provision, but the spiritual union of two people was never designed to be broken—the spirit is vulnerable in divorce and the pain continues. We may try to hide the pain that lingers from a broken spirit, but it's always there waiting for the opportunity to arise and consume us. Unless God rebuilds the foundation, those divorced often find themselves in the same situation with the second, third or fourth spouse.

> *The spiritual union of two people was never designed to be broken.*

The good news, however, is that both of the women spoke of God's healing power. Regardless of what they had endured, God delivered them from emotional scars. He can deliver those broken by a failed marriage as well, but *change must first occur on the inside.* Strongholds such as bitterness, pride, lust, past sexual experiences, selfishness, substance abuse, anger and physical abuse, to name a few, are among those that hinder the healing and rebuilding process. Healing begins with a commitment to work on those areas known to be detrimental to your spiritual health and relationships.

A commitment is just that—a commitment. Our attitude should be one in which we surrender our entire lifestyle to God. I've spoken with many who admitted that alcohol or substance abuse ruined their relationship, but instead of surrendering the problem to God and breaking their addiction, they simply found someone else to tolerate their habit. Unfortunately, the problem soon surfaced again. It's little wonder that many go through life changing partners, careers or residency, searching for someone or something that can never be found apart from spiritual wholeness. If this is you, I encourage you to stop wandering from relationship to relationship and allow a personal relationship with Jesus Christ to rebuild and restore you.

If you're like me, you may realize that years of "wandering" could have been avoided. Many, no doubt, had direction for their marriage, but because of selfishness, disobedience, disregard or a deaf ear to God's direction, it ended with divorce . . . but *God can rebuild and redeem that life;* He desires to guide and direct us.

> *The spirit of regret and failure will linger as long as we let it.*

Many who are currently separated or recently divorced can rebuild their marriage. However, far too many who are divorced are living in the past, failing to move forward—the spirit of regret and failure will linger as long as we let it.

God often uses brokenness to rebuild. An analogy that comes to mind is that of a shepherd. Perhaps you've heard that from time to time a shepherd might break the leg of a lamb that continually wandered from the flock, and thus, from the shepherd's protection. The shepherd would then splint the broken leg and carry the lamb on his shoulders for weeks until the leg had healed. As painful as this was for the lamb, it was necessary to protect it from being ravished by wolves or other predators. In time, through the broken and dependant relationship, the lamb learned to walk and to remain in the protective presence of his shepherd. This was well stated by David in Psalm 51:8, ". . . *That the bones You have broken may rejoice,*" and in Isaiah 53:6 "All we like sheep have gone astray . . ."

What will it take to bring us back to the Shepherd? A deliberate decision to stay close to Him can help us avoid needless pain, and provide safety and protection; this is the first step in changing brokenness into an unbreakable force.

DIVORCE: WHEN TO HOLD ON, WHEN TO MOVE ON

A major portion of this chapter was written during the single years that followed my divorce. It brought to mind the millions of people living with the consequences of a failed marriage; many may have desired to remain faithful to their commitment while their spouse chose to leave.

Life after divorce can be just "existence"—peace and joy have all but left. If this describes you, as it did me, let me assure you that God desires that peace and joy be restored. When my wife filed for divorce in 1998, as a single, I felt like half of a person that needed someone to complete me. In reality, a spouse will not complete me (or you); only God can bring wholeness and fullness to our lives. Don't believe the lie that you need someone in order to be complete. We were created as individuals, and God uses our individual qualities to glorify Him, married or single.

As mentioned earlier . . . you can't change where you've been, but you can change where you're going. I often thank the Lord for using my divorce to change my direction. God was not responsible for my divorce, but He did use it to redirect me—His nature is to redeem that which is lost. My divorce was the result of misguided focus, primarily on my part. That's why it's vitally important that two people enter the marriage covenant with the same spiritual belief system. Remember, the beliefs, goals and plans of two individuals are reflected in one relationship: marriage, where spiritual compatibility is critical. Do not lose your identity in the other person, but rather develop the gifts within your God-given individuality and learn to work together.

In my case, God used my situation to change me and bring new meaning to my life. Some of the consequences of my divorce may linger, but so will His unfailing grace, mercy and love, and for that I am continually grateful.

Clearly understand that I'm not advocating divorce, nor am I suggesting that if you are currently separated, divorce become an option because better opportunities await you. God hates divorce and anyone who has been there knows why. I believe, first and foremost, in reconciliation and restoration but these are not always options if both don't agree on reconciliation, or if extreme abuse exists. At this point, some may disagree and believe that Christian's are responsible to do whatever they can to reconcile. That's why a personal relationship with Jesus and access to His wisdom and daily guidance is profoundly important. Through that relationship you will be able to make the right decision as you answer the question whether to hold on or to move on. It won't be easy because lives have been damaged, dreams destroyed and promises broken, but God continually redeems us through His forgiveness. God desires that we get back on track and follow His lead in spite of detours.

DIVORCE—HOPE FOR THE HURTING

One of the biggest obstacles when considering restoration or seeking direction is becoming involved with someone soon after you divorce or separate. This can severely hinder your chance for reconciliation, as well as your ability to follow God's lead. You might feel that this new person makes you feel loved and appreciated, and that may be true, but so did your spouse when you first met. Again, *love does not leave people—people leave love, and until you've made changes that will change your future, you're bound to repeat your past.*

Every situation is different and some divorces are inevitable, but for the large percentage of those who can rebuild and restore their relationship, two choices are available, to face the pain of discipline, or the pain of regret. Disciplining yourself to do the right thing is difficult, but living with the pain of regret is much harder.

Although I accepted Christ at an early age, the pull of the world was enticing. I was influenced by how much money I made, what type of vehicle I wanted to own and where I wanted to live. As stated earlier, there is nothing wrong with having dreams, but there is a difference between having dreams and dreams having you.

There is a difference between having dreams and dreams having you.

As a result of my passion for worldly things, I entered into marriage with those things as first priorities and my marriage second, or third, or fourth. After four years of marriage, we succeeded financially but failed relationally. Immediately, we sought new relationships. Our focus shifted from a failed marriage to a new relationship; restoration became increasingly more difficult. If you are recently divorced, I encourage you not to move ahead in a new relationship until you have exhausted all avenues of restoration and a significant amount of time has passed. If you are separated, don't rush a divorce; and definitely do not begin a new relationship. Understand that you are about to make a big decision—a decision that will last a lifetime. Countless couples live with ongoing regret and remorse, simply because they trusted divorce for the answer rather than God and restoration. If you left an abusive relationship and have no plans of returning, there still needs to be time for healing, and a new relationship, more often than not, will only mask the pain, hinder the healing process and prevent problems from being addressed.

After spending a year searching for fulfillment through other relationships, I admitted to God that I was trying to find someone who would make me happy rather than focusing on what He wanted to do in me. I had no idea that it would take two additional years before He brought Morgan into my life. God was not only preparing someone for me, but me for them.

Perhaps my three-year journey could have been much longer had I not committed to change. Don't be like the Israelites and allow a short journey (a matter of days) through the wilderness to become forty-years of wandering; identify your weaknesses

Strengths are seen in what we stand for; weaknesses in what we fall for.

and commit to work on them. Strengths are seen in what we stand for; weaknesses in what we fall for. Identify your weaknesses, those areas that seem to trip you time-and-time again, and sincerely seek to make changes.

Is Restoration Always God's Will?

God hates divorce and reconciliation is pleasing to Him. There are instances when one is Scripturally released through adultery and is no longer bound, however it takes two to reconcile. First and foremost, God's will is that we walk in integrity, follow His principles and use wisdom during the journey. For some, reconciliation may result, for others it may not. Whether you are a divorced man or woman, God still loves you, and you can rebuild your life.

The enemy often resurrects past failures to prevent future success. He knows that God has plans for our lives and he

The enemy often resurrects past failures to prevent future success.

seeks to undermine those plans. For instance, as Morgan and I began our relationship, when I heard sermons about letting go of the past I would become excited about our new relationship, but when I heard discussions about divorce and restoration, I became fearful—my past was clearly preventing a hopeful future. But as we moved forward in the relationship, anxiety and confusion gave way to peace, joy and fulfillment.

As a final confirmation, before I committed fully to Morgan, I contacted my former wife (nearly three years after our divorce) to validate my feelings of being released from our past relationship. She confirmed that she was in a long-term relationship that would eventually lead to marriage, and she wished me the best. I felt that I had received my last and most solid confirmation. *It was now clear that I could no longer allow past brokenness to cause future pain.*

Morgan and I never fully understood why we felt anxiety; it did, however, cause us to focus more intently on God and not ourselves, and when we finally committed to our marriage vow, we knew it was a binding statement representing a life-long commitment—a commitment that we both had always wanted.

If you sense that restoration is possible, I encourage you to remove everything that may hinder this process such as wrong relationships, wrong attitudes, addictions or other strongholds. In addition, I highly recommend the two tape audio series from pastors Jack Hayford, Scott Bauer and John Tolle entitled: *The DEVASTATING Dimensions of Divorce.* The series is artfully presented and ministers to the needs of those recovering from divorce, those currently separated and those contemplating divorce. A question and answer segment is also included. (Their website address is www.livingway.com)

When To Hold On—When To Move On

The following pages were written to those who are questioning if they should hold on for restoration, or move on. Ultimately, only you, with God's help, can answer that question. It's my desire that this information will help you make the right decision. Before making a decision of this magnitude, I offer three directives.

1. First, discontinue any relationship that is not God-centered or that may cloud your judgment. (I often wonder how many marriages are not restored simply because people immediately become involved in other relationships and don't wait on the Lord.)

2. Second, pray, seek godly counsel and allow God's Word to direct you.

3. Third, don't be in a hurry. Restoration is a process. Don't abort the process because you're in a hurry. Healing and direction take time and patience. If it took years to damage the marriage, it may take years to rebuild, or for emotional wholeness to be restored.

FIVE POINTS TO CONSIDER . . .

1.   Perhaps the most difficult Scripture dealing with divorce or separation is found in 1 Corinthians 7:10–11 **". . . A wife must not leave her husband. But if she does leave him, let her remain single or else go back to him. And the husband must not leave the wife"** (NLT). This clearly states that those who are divorced and/or separated, unless "scripturally released", should not remarry. I believe that if this Scripture were fully acknowledged, it would be a deterrent to divorce and create more serious consideration before marriage and remarriage to another. There would be fewer divorces without cause and more reconciliations. Lack of regard for this Scripture has taken us to the other extreme—no fault divorce. However, if the spouse who left is an unbeliever and shows no desire for reconciliation after a significant amount of time, verse fifteen offers direction.

2.   1 Corinthians 7:15 states, **"But if the husband or wife who isn't a Christian insists on leaving, let them go. In such cases the Christian husband or wife is not required to stay with them, for God wants his children to live in peace"** (NLT). Even if this is the case, it's wise to allow a significant amount of time to pass before moving forward. This may reveal if the person left only for a season, or has chosen to leave permanently. Other translations of this verse state that a Christian is not under bondage in such a case. If someone leaves and has no intention of returning, God does not want us to be bound to that past relationship—He wants us to live in peace. In this case, I believe that marriage to another is an option, but as always, seek counsel and direction; always recognize God's Word as the ultimate source.

3.   Matthew 19:9 states **"And I tell you this, a man who divorces his wife and marries another commits adultery— unless his wife has been unfaithful"** (NLT). Again, God reveals His nature concerning commitment to a spouse. Clearly, a spouse who has been unfaithful releases the other and they are no longer bound. It is unfortunate that all divorced individuals are referred to as "divorced". It might be helpful and less confusing for those whose spouse was unfaithful to be referred to as "released". Certainly unfaithfulness does not mean that the marriage cannot be restored if both the husband and wife seek God's guidance.

4.   A personal favorite, 1 Corinthians 7:17 states, **"You must accept whatever situation the Lord has put you in, and continue on as you were when God first called you . . ."** (NLT). We are to use every situation for God's glory. If single, use that opportunity to build and strengthen character, and care for the things of God. If separated, use that time to seek God more fervently and pray for guidance and direction. Allow Him to mold and direct you, and rebuild the relationship. If divorced, use that experience to learn while asking what good can come from it; you may minister to others who have gone through a divorce. One of God's wonderful attributes is that He desires to use our brokenness. In fact, it is in our weakness that His strength is manifested. Be assured that all things can work together for good as we commit our lives to Him!

5.   **You can't control choices others make.** You may attempt to influence or encourage them, but ultimately the choice to leave or to stay is up to them. God has given us the freedom to choose; in marriage, the choices of one can greatly affect the life of the other. If you and your spouse are apart, and you've waited and done all that you

> *In marriage, the choices of one can greatly affect the life of the other.*

can do biblically, I believe that God looks at your heart more than your circumstance. King David was not able to build the temple because of his past—he was a man of war, but God said, ". . . Whereas it was in your heart to build a temple for My name, you did well in that it was in your heart" (II Chronicles 6:8); because David's heart was right, God counted it as righteousness. Although he did not build the temple, God looked upon him as if he had. In the same way, your marriage may not be restored, but as long as your heart is right, God will honor and bless your circumstances because you trusted in Him and were obedient. He can rebuild your life and open doors you might not have thought possible. Once I recommitted my life to Christ, it changed dramatically. I went from weekend alcohol consumption and a career that wasn't God-centered, to a life nearly void of alcohol cravings, a ministry I never dreamed possible and a godly wife who has been a tremendous blessing. Did I make bad decisions along the way? Yes, I did, but I was quick to repent and seek God's help. Had I become angry and unwilling to change, only the Lord knows where I'd be today. Choose wisely today because, again, the consequences of bad choices take us farther than we want to go, keep us longer than we want to stay and cost us more than we want to pay.

Seven Ways to Rebuild After Brokenness

As I was completing this chapter, I was asked to speak to a group of singles in Southern California. Ironically, the topic was *Rebuilding After Brokenness.* In prayerful preparation for this message, I isolated seven ways to rebuild based on the story of Nehemiah found in the Old Testament.

I. Fast and pray: Nehemiah 1:4 states, "So it was, when I heard these words, that I sat down and wept, and mourned for many days; I was fasting and praying before the God of heaven." Nehemiah discovered that the Jews who survived the captivity were living in great distress and that the wall of Jerusalem that had represented their strength had been destroyed. Nehemiah understood that the first step was prayer and fasting. *Fasting forces us to neglect the flesh and feed the spirit.* Fasting and prayer together release spiritual strength not otherwise available.

II. Confess: In verses six and seven Nehemiah prays, ". . . we have sinned against You. Both my father's house and I have sinned. We have acted very corruptly against You, and have not kept the commandments . . ." Although our brokenness may have resulted from the actions of another, we are never above reproach. Confession, prayer and fasting, are often beginning steps that open the door for God's restoring power.

> *Confession, prayer and fasting, are often beginning steps that open the door for God's restoring power.*

III. Return to God: This should be the first thing we do. In verses eight and nine, Nehemiah quotes God's commandment to Moses, ". . . If you are unfaithful, I will scatter you among the nations; but if you return to Me, and keep My commandments and do them, though some of you were cast out to the farthest part of the heavens, yet I will gather them from there, and bring them to the place which I have chosen as a dwelling for My name . . ." One of the leading causes of divorce in America is sexual unfaithfulness, but there is a solution. God reminds us that if we return to Him, and keep His commandments, He will bring us to a place of restoration. Whether we were the cause of the brokenness or were primarily on the receiving end, we must return to God and His commandments.

> *God reminds us that if we return to Him, and keep His commandments, He will bring us to a place of restoration.*

IV. **Position yourself to rebuild:** Nehemiah said to the king ". . . If it pleases the king, and if your servant has found favor in your sight, I ask that you send me to Judah, to the city of my fathers' tombs, that I may rebuild it" (2:5). Nehemiah didn't leave for Judah without first positioning himself by asking the king to bestow favor. He knew that he would need resources, men and the king's blessing to accomplish the task of rebuilding the wall. To position ourselves means *to align or arrange our lives in such a way that we are able to receive God's blessings.* During this step, remove everything that does not correspond with God's Word. For example, if you're praying for restoration in your marriage, or seeking a godly spouse, don't live promiscuously. If you're in the healing stages, resurrecting past memories and regrets is not wise—positioning yourself in the center of God's will is now your primary focus.

V. **Use new things to build:** In Nehemiah 2:8, we read that Nehemiah requested new lumber for the rebuilding of the wall, the gates and his home. Although he used old stones from the previous wall, Nehemiah also needed new material to rebuild the new wall. In the same way, God will bring new things into your life; be open to change. *How do you know when your past is affecting your future?* If your plans, hopes and dreams are drawing from the past and preventing change, your past may be affecting your future. For instance, for several months after I met Morgan, I was not able to move forward in our relationship. My divorce, although years earlier, was still haunting me. Morgan was the first woman I courted since my divorce, and trust and marital failure were issues I had to resolve before we moved forward—I needed to be open for change.

VI. **Hold it in your heart:** This step refers mainly to those who are in the critical restoration and rebuilding stages of a marriage. Nehemiah 2:12 states, "Then I arose in the night, I and a few men with me; I told no one what my God had put in my heart to do at Jerusalem . . ." When God places something in your spirit, *it's best not to disclose immediately,* simply ponder it in your heart. If you're sensing restoration in your spirit, at times, avoid sharing this with your ex-spouse just yet. A true story involved a wife who left her husband. During the separation, he called her nearly every day, sent dozens of flowers and wrote letters routinely telling her how God was going to restore their marriage. After nearly a year, his wife filed for divorce and moved away. When asked if she considered reconciliation, she stated that she considered it many times but because of his constant pressure for restoration, she felt stifled and inclined to move farther away. Dr. Dobson's book, *Love Must Be Tough,* refers to this as *opening the cage door.* When a spouse who feels smothered or fenced in wants to leave (or has left), it's wise to open the cage door and release him or her. Although not true of every situation, time away allows them to reconsider their marriage, and reconciliation may then become an option. The husband previously mentioned actually contributed to his wife's decision to leave by never opening the cage door. *Don't be a "velcro man" (or woman) in a relationship, a marriage or attempting to restore one—use wisdom and patience.*

VII. Expect opposition: As you begin to rebuild and restore your life expect opposition. Nehemiah 2:19 says, ". . . they laughed at us and despised us . . ." The enemy will oppose us any way that he can. He'll use pessimistic people and/or fill our minds with negative thoughts in an attempt to distract us from reaching our goal. Again, don't allow people's opinions to become your reality unless they are positive. Those trying to rebuild a marriage may be taunted by the thought, "It's useless—why try?" Those trying to rebuild a broken past may often think, "I've done too much damage—why try, God can't use me now." The enemy emphasizes the negative and attempts to conceal the positive. Nehemiah responded in verse twenty, ". . . the God of heaven Himself will prosper us; therefore we His servants will arise and build . . ." Nehemiah understood that *God Himself would oversee the building project regardless of the damage or the hostility.* Once Nehemiah overcame his critics, his opposition became even greater. Nehemiah 4:3 states ". . . Whatever they build, if even a fox goes up on it, he will break down their stone wall," and verse eight adds, "and all of them conspired together to come and attack Jerusalem and create confusion." Nehemiah's opposition increased as he continued to obey God. He understood that if God was for him no one could stand against him, and he eventually rebuilt the wall. Likewise, God is greater than the problem you're facing. The key is to focus on what He can and will do in your life even though no evidence is seen. Hebrews 11:1 reminds us that . . . "faith is the substance of things hoped for, the evidence of things not seen." Faith believes God's promises before they happen. Simply stated, stay focused on the goal not the opposition.

> *Stay focused on the goal not the opposition.*

As you rebuild, I encourage you to wait on the Lord, obey His Word, seek guidance through counsel and allow God to work in your life. Ask, trust and move forward. God's lead is usually not as direct as we'd like; however it is certain. Again, ask for wisdom and guidance and make sure that your decision agrees with Scripture, then take that step of faith.

The steps of faith fall on the seemingly void, but find the rock beneath (Whittier). You may feel that you're walking blindly in to the unknown, but as you step out and trust, you'll find the rock beneath.

> *The steps of faith fall on the seemingly void, but find the rock beneath.*
> —Whittier

QUESTIONS TO CONSIDER:

Do you agree that life can make us bitter or it can make us better, and that the choice is ultimately ours?

Death is a natural process, but the spiritual union of two people was never designed to be broken. If you are suffering from divorce, what steps can be taken to revitalize your broken spirit?

Until you've made changes that will change your future, you're bound to repeat your past. What changes in attitude and actions can prevent repeating past mistakes?

Do you agree that the enemy often resurrects past failures to prevent future success? Do you also agree that the choices we make today will influence the quality of our life tomorrow? How can you develop and/or maintain a positive attitude?

Memorize Philippians 3:13, ". . . but one thing I do, forgetting those things which are behind and reaching forward to those things which are ahead."

"The choice is up to us. Do we passively stand-by while marriages are being shattered and families destroyed, or do we engage the enemy and rebuild our nation on solid biblical ground? It's not too late. But before we can rebuild our nation, we must first restore the family; and before we restore the family, we must first strengthen the individual—it all begins with each of us."

—Shane Idleman, 2002

CHAPTER NINE

Solid Choices in Unstable Times

Seven Principles to Live By

As this book was nearing completion, we were discussing Morgan's dating experience and her addition to *What Works for Singles*. She jokingly said, "I can tell the readers what doesn't work!" On a more serious note, although this book explains the principles in detail, I asked her to briefly share her experience concerning each one.

Morgan Responds . . .

Like many, I made wrong choices during my single years, but I've since learned that applying biblical principles could have prevented many of my mistakes. Thankfully, as I began to obey God's Word, He brought meaning and a renewed passion to my life; however, I still had to deal with the consequences of my actions from earlier years.

My previous relationships had this in common—*they lacked peace because I walked outside of the safety and protection of God's covering.* When I began to date Shane, I was committed to stay within God's realm of security and shelter by applying fundamental, scriptural principles.

1. **Choosing to change from the inside out.** A Christian commitment required that I drastically change my mindset. We cannot successfully change our behavior without first changing the inner condition of our heart. Although I accepted Christ as my Savior when I was eighteen, it would take time to break certain patterns that had developed during my teen years. The changes God has made since are beyond measure. Don't overlook a personal relationship with Jesus Christ—it's through this relationship, and only through this relationship, that you will be able to build deeply fulfilling relationships and to assure something of eternal value for your life.

2. **Wisdom.** When I was twenty, I dated a man that I thought I might someday marry. My family, friends and even my pastor encouraged me to reconsider the relationship. Foolishly, I didn't heed their advice. I rushed the relationship and moved from my home in California to his family's home in the Midwest, and we were eventually engaged. After a few short months, I moved back home and cancelled the wedding. This burden and heartache could have been avoided had I used wisdom and patience in pursuing the relationship, and paid closer attention to the obvious red flags and the counsel of others.

SOLID CHOICES IN UNSTABLE TIMES

An important aspect of wisdom is seeking godly counsel, but seeking counsel can be difficult because we so desperately want to hear *what we want to hear.* I wanted the approval of others for marriage although I felt no peace. This time, however, I was committed to doing things right. Before Shane and I began courting, we involved our families and friends. I actually enjoyed this process because as I learned how well Shane was loved and respected, I had the freedom to "fall" a little more. If you're beginning a relationship or are currently involved in one, begin seeking godly counsel and continue to do so during the course of the relationship. Ask the Lord to show you, and your loved ones, any points of caution and whether or not you should move forward, then, patiently wait. Again, *you can rarely go wrong waiting, but you can often go wrong rushing!*

3. **Choose discipline over regret.** Why do we cringe at the sound of discipline? Probably because we associate it with doing something difficult, when in reality, discipline simply means putting into action the right choice. It is one of the most important character qualities

we possess—it allows us to control our actions rather than allowing our actions to control us. I have learned that the results of choosing discipline far outweigh the consequences that come with lasting regret. Ask yourself this simple question before you make a decision that may compromise your values, *"Do I want to experience the temporary pain of discipline or the lasting pain of regret?"* The answer will be clear.

4. **Preparation.** Prior to meeting Shane, I struggled daily with jealousy, and still do at times. Inevitably, my thoughts began to hinder our relationship. I realized that I could no longer label it a struggle—it had become a lifestyle. I felt as if I was trapped in a bubble, looking at the outside world, longing to be free. As Shane stated before, *we should first learn to be a blessing before we seek one.* It is true that we're often so anxious to meet "the one" that we don't work on becoming "the one." We often bring unnecessary baggage into relationships when, in fact, we should be lightening this load ahead of time. Thankfully, Shane is learning to pray for me rather than to get angry, to understand rather than become impatient, and to love unconditionally rather than walk away. Within this secure and nurturing framework, I am free to be who I am while continuing to develop spiritual character. If you're aware of any issues that may prevent the development of a healthy relationship, I encourage you to begin working on them now and save your marriage before it begins.

5. **Making the right choice.** Like many girls, I began taking an interest in boys when I was in fifth grade, and by the time I was fifteen I was involved in a serious relationship. Had I known it would serve as the catalyst for other hurtful relationships, a deep mistrust of men, a distorted view of sex and low self-esteem, I believe that I would have reconsidered my options. That relationship clouded my vision and set the pace for more wrong choices. I reminded myself of a chameleon, changing my personality to suit each new relationship. It wasn't until I was preparing for marriage that I would fully understand the damaging effects of those wrong choices.

When we follow God's plan for our lives, we invite trust and stability into our relationships; we also have the advantage of knowing that we are making the decision to marry based on character qualities rather than on passion. There was spiritual wholeness and a renewed commitment to purity that Shane and I were able to bring into our relationship. Although there are negative consequences for poor choices, there are also positive consequences for wise choices. Focus on purity regardless of your past—it's still worth the wait!

6. **First things first.** I needed to revisit the emphasis I placed on career. I had been successfully pursuing an acting career, but as I grew spiritually, I found that the most important titles are those of a wife and a mother, not actress, businesswoman or professional, although I have to remind myself of that at times. Today's culture defines being a housewife and a mother as unimportant, but God tells us otherwise. Be who the Lord wants you to be and He will bring true satisfaction. If you are a wife or a mother, place your family first—the fulfillment of other interests can come with time. The focus should be on gaining a right perspective on God, family and career, and in that order. I'm still pursuing the desires of my heart; the difference is that I'm learning to prioritize.

7. **Character.** Looking back, I hardly recognize the girl I once was because of the amazing work God has done by turning my past regrets into a future full of hope; much of this was done by developing my character. Don't get discouraged; character is built from the struggles we face and the difficulties we overcome. Good character reflects integrity, restores relationships and influences others to look to God for support and encouragement. Our words, our actions and our habits all reflect our character. Continually look to God's Word for examples of character and integrity. His laws are there to protect us, not to prevent us from enjoying life.

QUESTIONS TO CONSIDER BEFORE MARRIAGE

How Well Do You Know Your Potential Spouse?

Many know little about each other before they marry; therefore, this simple checklist was included. Know your future spouse before feelings are hurt over even the smallest things such as how you celebrate birthdays or who does the dishes. It's best to define expectations and learn as much as you can about one another before making one of the biggest decisions of your life. Not all questions may be appropriate for dating—you decide. Feel free to add to the list.

Whose Responsibility Is It To . . .

1. Balance the books?

2. Pay the bills?

3. Clean the house?

4. Keep up the landscaping?

5. Oversee household and automobile repairs?

6. Do laundry?

7. Lock the doors and turn off the lights at night?

8. Cook dinner?

9. Empty the trash?

10. Help with homework?

11. Oversee car and household repairs?

Add other responsibilities for discussion:

General Questions . . .

1. Will both of you work?

2. If both work, who cares for the children when they arrive?

3. How many children would you like?

4. How do you define your role as a parent.

5. Will you home-school your children, pay for private schooling or enroll them in a public school?

6. What church, if any, will you attend and why?

7. Do you prefer to live in the suburb or the country?

8. Describe an ideal vacation?

9. How do you spend the holidays?

10. How do you spend weekends?

11. How much time should you spend together?

12. How is your attitude in general (e.g., defensive, passive, aggressive, compliant, resistant, etc.)?

13. What style and colors do you like for your home (exterior and interior)?

14. As your parents age, will you place them in a home or care for them yourself?

15. How will you manage your money? Will there be a budget? If so, based on what income?

16. Will you tithe?

17. Are you a saver or a spender?

18. Do you agree to discuss all topics openly and honestly?

19. What hurts your feelings in private and in public?

20. When you are getting uncomfortable with a conversation among others, what "secret signal" can you arrange in advance between the two of you?

21. When talking with friends and family, what topics should be avoided (e.g., income, arguments, sex, etc.)?

22. How long should a couple date and/or court before they marry? How long should the engagement last?

23. What might be your greatest challenge in marriage? Why?

24. What family traditions do you hold dear?

25. Do you like to entertain?

26. Do you like crowds, company or visitors? Discuss various situations.

27. How will your views on politics affect the relationship? Which political party do you support? Why?

28. What are your feelings on topics such as abortion, stem-cell research, same sex marriage, sex before marriage, sex after marriage and pregnancy? (Note: as the relationship progresses, topics such as STD's and sexual problems should be discussed prior to a serious commitment.)

29. Describe your ideal (but realistic) marriage expectations—roles, rules, vacations, hobbies, and involvements.

Can you think of other questions to discuss?

Family Experiences

1. Your early years.

2. Your father's role/your mother's role.

3. What you learned from your childhood experience.

4. Other experiences that you would like to discuss.

5. How your childhood was overall.

6. How you view life overall.

7. Your teen and young adult years using the previous questions.

8. If and when you committed your life to Christ; discuss your experience.

9. Your most painful memories/the happiest times in your life.

10. What you will do like your mother, like your father.

11. How you will be un-like your mother, un-like your father.

12. How can you apply what you have learned from their lives?

In closing, state what you value most in your partner, and what you will do to encourage that virtue and support their growth.

Other resources from *El Paseo Publications*,
including the book and audio series
WHAT WORKS When "Diets" Don't,
and ***What Works for Men,***
are available through
www.whydietsdontwork.com or
www.elpaseopublications.com

Notes

Chapter One:

1. FOCUS ON THE FAMILY, September 2002 newsletter. Data from the National Survey of Family and Households.

2. Readers Digest, September–October 2002.

3. Turning Point Ministries, *Insight Group—group member guide*, 1989, 1992, 1995.

4. George Barna and Mark Hatch, *Boiling Point: It Only Takes One Degree,* 2001—published by Gospel Light.

5. David Barton, *America—to pray or not to pray*, 1995—published by WallBuilder Press.

6. Dr. Ted Broer's radio interview entitled: *Top Ten Foods Never to Eat,* copyright 2002.

7. The Three-in-one Concise—*Bible reference companion*—Bible reference companion, published by Nelson 1982.

8. *The Funk and Wagnalls Standard Desk Dictionary,* 1986 edition, published by Funk and Wagnalls.

Chapter Two:

1. Coral Ridge Ministries website, statistics on abortion, 2002.

2. David Barton, *America—to pray or not to pray, 1995—*published by WallBuilder Press.

3. *The WallBuilder Report*, Spring 2002.

4. Ted Broer, *Maximum Energy*, 1999—published by Siloam Press.

5. Ted Broer, *EAT, DRINK & be HEALTHY AUDIO SERIES*, 2002.

6. Shane Idleman, *WHAT WORKS When "Diet's" Don't*, 2002—published by El Paseo Publications.

7. Don Rannikar, *Choosing God's Best*, published by Multnomah, 1998.

8. The Three-in-one Concise—Bible reference companion, published by Nelson 1982.

9. Tommy Nelson, *The Book of Romance,* 1998—published by Thomas Nelson.

10. *The Funk and Wagnalls Standard Desk Dictionary,* 1986 edition, published by Funk and Wagnalls.

Chapter Three:

1. The Three-in-one Concise—Bible reference companion, published by Nelson 1982.

2. Shane Idleman, *WHAT WORKS When "Diet's" Don't*, 2002— published by El Paseo Publications.

3. *The Funk and Wagnalls Standard Desk Dictionary,* 1986 edition, published by Funk and Wagnalls.

Chapter Four:

1. John C. Maxwell, *Failing Forward,* 2000—published by Nelson, 2000.

2. The Three-in-one Concise—Bible reference companion, published by Nelson, 1982.

3. FOCUS on the Family magazine, 2002.

4. George Barna and Mark Hatch, *Boiling Point: It Only Takes One Degree,* 2001—published by Gospel Light.

5. *The Funk and Wagnalls Standard Desk Dictionary,* 1986 edition, published by Funk and Wagnalls.

Chapter Five:

1. The Three-in-one Concise—Bible reference companion, published by Nelson, 1982.

2. Don Rannikar, *Choosing God's Best*, published by Multnomah, 1998.

3. Bishop T.D. Jakes at San Quinton Prison *(Tape Series: Prison Breaking Truths).*

4. Bishop T.D. Jakes, *I'll Never Do That Again-The Temptation Series, 2002.*

5. Dr. James Dobson, *Love For A Lifetime*, published by Multnomah, 1987, 1993, 1996, 1998.

6. John C. Maxwell, *Failing Forward*, published by Nelson, 2002.

7. *The Funk and Wagnalls Standard Desk Dictionary*, 1986 edition, published by Funk and Wagnalls.

Chapter Six:

1. Bob Demoss, *TV The Great Escape;* interview on Family Life Today.

2. The Three-in-one Concise—Bible reference companion, published by Nelson, 1982.

3. Shane Idleman, *WHAT WORKS When "Diet's" Don't*, 2002—published by El PaseoPublications.

4. *The Funk and Wagnalls Standard Desk Dictionary*, 1986 edition, published by Funk and Wagnalls.

Chapter Seven:

1. Edgar A. Guest, *The Light of Faith*, published by Reily and Lee Co. 1926.

2. *The Seven Deadly Sins of Bible Study*, online feature for New Man Magazine, 6/11/02.

3. William Martin, *A PROPHET WITH HONOR*: *The Billy Graham Story,* published by Quill, 1991.

4. The Three-in-one Concise—Bible reference companion, published by Nelson, 1982.

5. David Barton, *America—to pray or not to pray*, 1995—published by WallBuilder Press.

6. Rick Warren, *The Purpose Driven Life,* published by Zondervan, 2002.

7. Jack Hayford, *Pursuing The Will of God*, published by Living Way Ministries, 1997, 2002.

8. Charles Stanley, *Charles Stanley's handbook for Christian Living*, published by Thomas Nelson, 1996.

9. Charles R. Swindoll, *Living Above the Level of Mediocrity,* published by Word Books, 1987.

10. *The Funk and Wagnalls Standard Desk Dictionary*, 1986 edition, published by Funk and Wagnalls.

Chapter Eight:

1. Craig Barnes, *Sacred Thirst*, published by Zondervan, 2000.

2. The Three-in-one Concise—Bible reference companion, published by Nelson 1982.

3. Jack Hayford, Scott Bauer and John Tolle. *Tape series entitled: The DEVASTATING Dimensions of Divorce* (SC 408).

4. Weldon Phillip Keller, *A Shepherd Looks at Psalm 23,* published by Zondervan 1970.

5. James C. Dobson, *Love Must Be Tough,* published by Word Publishing Group, 1996.

6. *The Funk and Wagnalls Standard Desk Dictionary,* 1986 edition, published by Funk and Wagnalls.

JOURNAL NOTES

*Date*_____

JOURNAL NOTES

*Date*_____

JOURNAL NOTES

*Date*_____

JOURNAL NOTES

*Date*_____

_____

_____

_____

_____

_____

_____

_____

_____

_____

_____

_____

_____

_____

_____

_____

_____

_____

_____

_____

_____

_____

_____

_____

_____

_____

_____

JOURNAL NOTES

*Date*_____

JOURNAL NOTES

*Date*_____

JOURNAL NOTES

*Date*_____

JOURNAL NOTES

*Date*_____

_____

_____

_____

_____

_____

_____

_____

_____

_____

_____

_____

_____

_____

_____

_____

_____

_____

_____

_____

_____

_____

_____

_____

_____

_____

_____

_____

_____

_____

JOURNAL NOTES

*Date*_____

JOURNAL NOTES

*Date*_____

_____

_____

_____

_____

_____

_____

_____

_____

_____

_____

_____

_____

_____

_____

_____

_____

_____

_____

_____

_____

_____

_____

_____

_____

_____

_____

_____

JOURNAL NOTES

*Date*_____

JOURNAL NOTES

*Date*_____

JOURNAL NOTES

*Date*_____

JOURNAL NOTES

*Date*_____

JOURNAL NOTES

*Date*_____

JOURNAL NOTES

*Date*_____

JOURNAL NOTES

*Date*_____

JOURNAL NOTES

*Date*_____

JOURNAL NOTES

*Date*_____

JOURNAL NOTES

*Date*_____

JOURNAL NOTES

*Date*_____

JOURNAL NOTES

*Date*_____

JOURNAL NOTES

*Date*_____

JOURNAL NOTES

*Date*_____

JOURNAL NOTES

*Date*_____

JOURNAL NOTES

*Date*_____

JOURNAL NOTES

Date_____

JOURNAL NOTES

*Date*_____

JOURNAL NOTES

*Date*_____

JOURNAL NOTES

*Date*_____

_____

_____

_____

_____

_____

_____

_____

_____

_____

_____

_____

_____

_____

_____

_____

_____

_____

_____

_____

_____

_____

_____

_____

_____

_____

_____

JOURNAL NOTES

*Date*_____

JOURNAL NOTES

*Date*_____

JOURNAL NOTES

*Date*_____

JOURNAL NOTES

*Date*_____

_____

_____

_____

_____

_____

_____

_____

_____

_____

_____

_____

_____

_____

_____

_____

_____

_____

_____

_____

_____

_____

_____

_____

_____

_____

_____

_____

_____

JOURNAL NOTES

*Date*_____

JOURNAL NOTES

*Date*_____

_____

_____

_____

_____

_____

_____

_____

_____

_____

_____

_____

_____

_____

_____

_____

_____

_____

_____

_____

_____

_____

_____

_____

_____

_____

_____

JOURNAL NOTES

*Date*_____

JOURNAL NOTES

*Date*_____